The Wisdom of the Gita

...A Manual for Life

J.M. Mehta

Published by

An Imprint of
Pustak Mahal®, Delhi
J-3/16 , Daryaganj, New Delhi-110002
☎ 23276539, 23272783, 23272784 • *Fax:* 011-23260518
E-mail: info@pustakmahal.com • *Website:* www.pustakmahal.com

London Office
5, Roddell Court, Bath Road, Slough SL3OQ J, England
E-mail: pustakmahaluk@pustakmahal.com

Sales Centre
10-B, Netaji Subhash Marg, Daryaganj, New Delhi-110002
☎ 23268292, 23268293, 23279900 • *Fax:* 011-23280567

Branch Offices
Bangalore: ☎ 22234025
E-mail: pmblr@sancharnet.in • pustak@sancharnet.in
Mumbai: ☎ 22010941
E-mail: rapidex@bom5.vsnl.net.in
Patna: ☎ 3094193 • *Telefax:* 0612-2302719
E-mail: rapidexptn@rediffmail.com
Hyderabad: *Telefax:* 040-24737290
E-mail: pustakmahalhyd@yahoo.co.in

© Copyright : Hindoology Books
ISBN 978-81-223-0914-0
Edition : September 2007

The Copyright of this book, as well as all matter contained herein (including pictures) rests with the Publishers. No person shall copy the name of the book, its title design, matter and illustrations in any form and in any language, totally or partially or in any distorted form. Anybody doing so shall face legal action and will be responsible for damages.

Printed at : Param Offsetters, Okhla, New Delhi-110020

Preface

The Gita holds a unique position among the ancient scriptures of the world. Numerous commentaries have already been written on the Gita. However, despite its great importance, its living truths have not reached the teeming millions in India, who consider it more as an object of worship and reverence. Some excellent books written by outstanding and eminent persons have become either reference books in libraries or show-pieces in elite houses, educational and religious institutions. These books are also voluminous and high-priced and hence beyond the interest and access of an average Indian. Consequently the real teachings of the Gita have not percolated down the common masses.

Inspite of several books already available in the market, the humble writer of this book has a distinct purpose in bringing out yet another. This purpose is to help spread the wisdom of the Gita, among average English-knowing reader, by presenting a small, low-priced, easily understandable book, simple in language, succint in approach and having a direct bearing on every-day life.

I have no knowledge of sanskrit which is the language of the original text. My acquaintance with the Gita has been through books written in English and Hindi, besides through talks and lectures heard in these languages. The thoughts contained in this book have been compiled on the basis of what I have read, heard, analysed and understood according to my capacity and limitations.

I also wish to add that I have no claim to erudition or originality in interpretation of these thoughts. Of course, I have tried to put these thoughts in a manner and language of my choice.

Having stumbled through vicissitudes of everyday life, I sincerely felt that there should be some compact guidelines to run through the rigours of life. One can hardly find better guidelines than those contained in the teachings of the Gita. The Gita transcends the boundaries of race, religion or country and contains divine wisdom, is beneficial for all mankind and for all times. It can help human beings in solving ever-existing problems of ignorance and bondage, love and hate, duty and action and so on. The Gita teaches the fundamentals of true religion, and as a fountain spring of wisdom, can serve as a manual for life, for all people, at all times.

—J.M. Mehta
New Delhi

Contents

Some Famous Comments on The Gita   7

The Gita — Some Interesting Facts   10

The Background   11

The Gita — A Manual for Life   13

The Mystery of Life   15

The Goal of Life   17

Courage in Crisis   20

Do not Fear Death, Do not Grieve   22

Pleasure and Pain   25

Yoga as Defined in The Gita   28

Karma Yoga (Path of Action)   33

Nishkam Karma (Selfless Action)   39

Gyan Yoga (Path of Knowledge)   41

Bhakti Yoga (Path of Devotion)   44

Synthesis of Yoga   48

Three Types of Gunas   50

Three-fold Classification   53

Four-fold Order of Society   57

Renunciation and Relinquishment 60

Devotees of God 63

Good and Evil Tendencies 65

The Field and Its Knower 69

Desires 74

God and Nature 79

Functioning and Control of Mind 82

Meditation 86

Incarnation of God 89

Selected Memorable Verses 90

A Summary of Prominent Teachings of The Gita 102

Epilogue 107

Some Famous Comments on The Gita

The Gita is a bouquet composed of the beautiful flowers of spiritual truths collected from the Upanishads.
—Swami Vivekananda

The Gita is the universal mother. I find solace in the Gita which I miss even in the sermon on the mount. When disappointment stares me in the face and all alone, I see not one ray of light, I go back to the Gita. I find a verse here and a verse there, and immediately begin to smile in the midst of overwhelming tragedies.
—Mahatma Gandhi

In the whole world of literature, there is no book so elevating and inspiring as the Gita. It is the source of all wisdom. It is your greatest guide. It is your supreme teacher. It is an inexhaustible spiritual treasure. It is an ocean of knowledge. It is a universal scripture for people of all temperaments and for all times.
—Swami Sivananda

The Gita was preached in order to give philisophical advice as to how one should live one's worldly life, with an eye to release the true duty of human beings in worldly life.
—B.G. Tilak

Its teaching is acknowledged as of the highest value. Its influence is not merely philosophic or academic but immediate and living, an influence both for thought and action, and its ideas are actually at work as a powerful shaping factor in the renewal of a nation and a culture.

—*Aurobindo Ghosh*

It is a means to lift the aspirant from the lower levels of renunciation, where objects are renounced, to the loftier heights, where desires are dead, and where the yogi dwells in calm and ceaseless contemplation, which his body and mind are acrively employed in, discharging the duties that fall to his lot in life. It is a scripture of yoga which means harmony with the Divine law, becoming one with the Divine life, by the subdual of all outward going agencies.

—*Annie Besant*

The Gita is one of the clearest and most comprehensive summaries of the Perennial Philisophy, ever to have been done. Hence its enduring values are not only for Indians, but for all mankind.

—*Aldous Huxley*

The Gita is a handbook of instructions as to how every human being can come to live the subtle philosophical principles of Vedanta in the actual world. This is a great handbook of practical living.

—*Swami Chinmayananda*

The Bhagwad Gita is a valuable aid for the understanding of the supreme ends of life.

—*Dr. S. Radha Krishnan*

The Bhagwad Gita is one of the world-scriptures today. It guides the life of people all over the world.

—*Divine Life Society*

Sung by Lord Krishna, the Gita, drenched in ambrosial compassion, is the provider of initiation into duty, lessons of equanimity, alms of englightenment and surrender, and is for the welfare of the mankind.

—*Swami Ramsukh Das Ji*

The Bhagwad Gita is a technique for dynamic living and not a retirement plan.

—*Swami Parthasarthy*

❐❐

The Gita – Some Interesting Facts

- The full name is BHAGWAD GITA — which means the song of the Lord.
- The original text is in SANSKRIT — which is the oldest language and is considered as the mother of several languages.
- It is the greatest, poetical, spiritual discourse ever given in the history of mankind.
- It is believed that this discourse was given by LORD KRISHNA (believed to be incarnation of God) to his disciple and friend ARJUNA, around 5000 years ago.
- It is an intrinsic part of the epic of 'MAHABHARATA' and its authorship is attributed to RISHI VED VYASA.
- The Gita consists of eighteen chapters, containing a total of 700 VERSES *(Shlokas)*. Arjuna spoke 84 *shlokas*, while Lord Krishna spoke 514 *shlokas*. The rest were by others.
- Numerous commentaries have been written on the Gita. The commentary by SANKARA is considered as the most ancient of the existing ones.
- The Gita has been translated into most languages of the world.

❏❏

The Background

The war of Mahabharata, which was fought between the cousins, Kauravs and Pandavs, at the battleground of Kurukshetra, serves as a background to the Gita. This war was caused because of the arrogance of the Kaurav prince Duryodhana, who refused to part with even a small territory of the kingdom to the Pandavs for their living and sustenance. The rival armies led by Duryodhana and Arjuna faced each other at Kurukshetra. Lord Krishna, a friend and guide of Arjuna, acted as his charioteer. At the crucial moment, when the two armies stood ready before the battle, Arjuna requested Krishna to place his chariot in the midst of both the armies so that he can survey the battlefield. When Krishna complied, Arjuna found that his respected elders, teachers, close relatives and friends were all arrayed against him. Observing this grim reality, he was overwhelmed at the thought of killing his own kith and kin. He, therefore, felt great sorrow and deep depression and told Krishna thus:

"I covet no victory, riches or kingdom and do not want to kill them even though they kill me."

Having spoken this, Arjuna laid down his arms and sat down in his chariot, stricken with grief and depression. In this scenario, Lord Krishna delivered the sermon of the Gita to Arjuna, removed his doubts and depression and ultimately prepared him for the fight.

The story of the Mahabharata, which has been portrayed as an epic battle has wider philisophical significance for the mankind. The battle which was fought at Kurukshetra is a pointer towards a battle on the mental and spiritual level being fought in the human mind, at all times. It is a battle between good and evil tendencies, duties and desires; noble and ignoble actions. The Pandavas and the Kaurvas who represent good and evil forces respectively., may be compared to positive and negative tendencies of an individual. A constant conflict is ever going on between higher and lower natures of an individual.

The Gita represents a symbolic picture of life's continuous battle. The problems faced by Arjuna are not individualistic. They are of universal nature. The crisis of choice of right and wrong which confronted Arjuna, is faced by every individual, in some form or the other. Arjuna is a representative person of his age. Kurukshetra is not just a historical battlefield or place. It symbolises the field of action in everyday life of each individual. This eternal and universal life situation, in the form of battle of life, forms the real background of the Gita.

❑❑

The Gita – A Manual for Life

Human life would certainly become worth-living and beneficial if one knows the basic principles to deal with its different aspects. One can know these principles either from a man of wisdom and true knowledge or from a holy book like the Gita, which contains and teaches such knowledge. The vast domain of the Gita provides knowledge about the perishable body, the immortal soul, human faculties, life and death, God and universe, pleasure and pain, action and duty, good and evil, yoga, meditation, devotion and mental attitudes which determine human nature and behaviour. This list is only indicative and not exhaustive. Almost every chapter of the Gita, if rightly understood and practised will help in moulding life on the right path. The Gita provides instructions to control mind, to achieve true knowledge and lasting peace and also shows the way to deal with doubt, despair, fear and anxiety – such instances which are so abundant in every day life.

The real aim of the Gita is to uplift humanity from ignorance of the material existence. Each individual in this world is entangled in difficulties which cause pain and suffering. The teachings of the Gita can guide him to find a way out of these adverse situations. By explaining the reality of God, soul and ever-changing nature, it tells us the fundamental truths which intertwine human life.

We are living in the age of science which brings various advantages and can cause tremendous misery also. As an agent of power, it does not know what is wrong or right. The awareness of right and wrong can be provided only through ideas prepounded by great thinkers and spiritual teachers. The Gita is an invaluable source of these very ideas which indicate, support and propogate moral and spiritual values.

The essential purpose of the Gita is to teach us a way out of ignorance and bondage which are the real cause of human misery. It explains the meaning of existence and the goal of life. The Gita teaches the yogas of action, knowledge and devotion. It teaches faith, divinity and glory of God, discrimination between good and bad tendencies and modes which can influence human conduct and personality. The practical way of living in the world, through Karma Yoga or selfless action is indicated in the Gita.

In short, the Gita can act as an unfailing guide in life, as it shows the way through thick and thin; midst joy and sorrow; in pleasure and pain and in moments of doubts and despair and much more.

The Gita is a wise companion, and a sure guide for the journey of life. It is indeed a manual which provides guidelines for righteous living.

❏❏

The Mystery of Life

Most of us do not know what life is all about? For an average person, life is the short span between birth and death. The first day of life starts with the birth and death brings the last day of life. This is only a short-sighted view of life and does not convey the whole reality.

The Gita tells us that there was life before birth and it also continues, thereafter. It continues in different manner and forms and death in the present state of our existence is not the final destination. In this context, **Verse 12** of **Chapter II** of Gita is quoted as follows :

> "Never was there a time, when I was not, nor thou, nor these lords of men, nor will there ever be a time hereafter when we will all cease to be."

The above verse corroborates that life is perpetual and eternal.

What is life?

Broadly speaking, life is a combination of body, which is inert matter and soul which is a conscious life element. Soul being a subtle entity can not function by itself and therefore needs a medium through which it can operate. The soul, therefore, has to seek the aid of the physical body which inter-alia, has senses, mind and intelligence. The body is essential for performing actions in life. However the real master is the life element, or the individual self, called the soul.

The Gita clearly explains the difference between the body and the soul. In this context, it may be relevant to quote the following *Verses* from the Gita:

Verse 20 – Chapter II
"It is never born, nor does it die at any time, nor having come to be will again cease to be. Unborn, eternal, permanent and primeval. It is not slain when the body is slain."

Verse 22 – Chapter II
"Just as a person casts off worn-out garments and puts on other that are new, even so does the embodied soul casts off worn-out bodies and takes on that are new."

Verse 24 – Chapter II
"It is uncleavable. It can not be burnt and can neither he wetted or dried. It is eternal, all-pervading, unchanging and stead-fast. It is the same forever."

The above verses distinguish between body and soul and also clearly indicate that life is perpetual. The soul which is the driving force of life never dies; it is the body which perishes. As the soul takes on a new body after death, the life moves on from one span to another.

Caged in its physical frame, the soul gets into bondage because of ignorance and attachment with the external world through the media of senses and the mind. This process continues from one life to another. However, our present span of life offers an opportunity to the soul to get out of bondage and reach its ultimate goal of God realisation. As this ultimate goal may not be achieved in a single span of life, there are series of such spans which are regulated through numerous births and deaths in different shapes and forms of life.

The Gita describes the various paths through which the individual soul can attain its goal through Yoga, by constant practice, self-discipline and non-attachment.

The Goal of Life

Several *Verses* in the Gita indicate that God-realisation is the goal of human life.

The first indication is given in **Verse 15** of **Chapter II** as follows :

"The man who remains the same in pain and pleasure, who is wise makes himself fit for eternal life."

Self control and wisdom lead to eternal life which seems to be the goal. Since God is eternal, to be one with him or to know him is the ultimate aim of life.

There are other *Verses* in *Chapter II* which mention other probable goals, such as, attainment of purity of spirit which ends all sorrow, peace which leads to happiness and divine bliss. A similar thought is echoed in **Verse 10** of **Chapter IV,** as follows :

"Delivered from passion, fear and anger, absorbed in Me, taking refuge in Me, many purified by the austerity of widsom, have attained to My state of being."

The final aim seems to be to reach God. Again *Verse 24* of the same chapter mentions that God is to be attained by him who realises God in his actions.

That to reach God is the sole aim, is mentioned repeatedly in the Gita, as may be seen from the following *Verses* :

Verse 17 – Chapter V
"Thinking of that, directing their whole conscious being to that, making that their whole aim, with that as the sole object of their devotion, they reach a state from which, there is no return, their sins washed away by wisdom."

Verse 24 – Chapter V
"He who finds his happiness within, his joy within and likewise his light within, that again becomes divine and attains to the beatitude of God."

Verse 25 – Chapter V
"The holy men whose sins are destroyed, whose doubts are cut asunder, whose minds are disciplined and who rejoice in good to all creatures, attain to the beatitude of God."

Verse 15 – Chapter VI
"The yogi of subdued mind, ever keeping himself harmonised, attains to peace, the supreme nirvana, which abides in Me."

Verse 45 – Chapter VI
"But the yogi, who strives with assiduity cleansed of all sins, perfecting himself through many lives, then attains to the highest goal."

The highest goal mentioned above, apparently is to reach God. A similar thought is echoed in **Verse 10** of **Chapter X**, as follows :

"To those who are constantly devoted and worship Me with love, I grant the concentration of understanding by which they come to Me."

Clearly God is the goal which can be achieved through constant love and devotion. The same idea is expressed in the concluding *Chapter (XVIII)* of the Gita, as indicated in the verses quoted below :

Verse 65 – Chapter XVIII
"Fix thy mind on Me; be devoted to Me; sacrifice to Me; prostrate thy self before Me; so shall thou come to Me."

Verse 66 – Chapter XVIII
"Abandoning all duties, come to Me alone for shelter. Be not grieved, for I shall release thee from all evils".

It may be concluded from what has been stated above, that the same idea has been explained in several ways. Whether it is highest perfection, highest peace, freedom from all sorrows or evils, freedom from bondage, liberation of soul, purity of the spirit, reaching the Supreme the Absolute, the life eternal, the beatitude of God or some other similar state – all pointers lead to the same conclusion. The goal of life, therefore, may be summed up as God-realisation, which is the highest stage of spiritual attainment, beyond which there is nothing else to be attained.

❏❏

Courage in Crisis

The first chapter of the Gita deals with the scene of battlefield at Kurukshetra, where the battle of Mahabharata was fought. In the first verse of the chapter, Kurukshetra has been described as *Dharmakshetra* — which meant the field of *Dharma* or righteousness. This is symbolic of the battle of life which represents a moral struggle, a struggle between right and wrong, a struggle between good and evil. This chapter also describes the state of depression of Arjuna who overwhelmed by sorrow, casts away his bow and arrow and thus refuses to fight.

The real teachings of the Gita start with **Chapter II, Verse 3**, where Lord Krishna tells Arjuna :

"Yield not to this unmanliness for it does not become thee. Cast off this petty faint heartedness and arise.."

The above instruction is in response to the state of depression of Arjuna, who was overwhelmed with grief, at the prospect of killing his kith and kin and respected teachers.

In this set-up, Lord Krishna exhorts Arjuna not to yield to any weakness in the face of crisis and face the challange.

This is the first practical lesson from the Gita and is meant for the struggling humanity. The message is loud and clear — not to dishearten in the face of any difficult situation. The right course is to face the crisis and cope with difficulties of life with courage, strength and manliness. There is no scope for weakness in the battle of life which takes place, every moment, in the mind of men. This battle for a moral struggle has to be fought with courage and determinaton. This is the first clear message for everybody — to deal with difficult situations with courage at all times.

We must also understand — What is courage? Here are a few thoughts in this connection. Courage is a power to overcome danger, fear, misfortune, injustice, and affirming faith in the goodness of life on the ground and God overhead! It is a virtue of the brave who fight for a just cause in the face of physical challanges and hardships. Courage helps in overcoming fear, facing difficulties and meeting a challenge and in dealing with new situations and experiences beyond our expectations. It is easier to lose hope and run away in the face of crisis than to arise, stand up and face difficulties with courage. The message of the Gita in such situations of everyday life is:

"Have courage. face the crisis and do not discourage or run away.".

❐❐

Do not Fear Death, Do not Grieve

For a large number of people, life is a general drama of pain and grief, with an episode of happiness here and there, in between. The spectre of death haunts almost all beings in this world. Only a few brave individuals who are aware of the reality of death are not afraid. In general, most of us are afraid of death, at different stages of life, if not always in a lesser or greater degree. Human beings also feel sad and tormented on the passing away of their kith and kin, friends, well-wishers and sometimes even for strangers. At times and for some, the loss of a dear relative or a friend becomes extremely painful and unbearable. In some cases the sadness and grief over a tragic loss extends over a long period and even throughout life. This is only a small description of fear and consequences of death.

Now let us consider how the topics of grief and fear of death are dealt with in the Gita.

Verse 11 of *Chapter II* of the Gita is relevant and noteworthy. In this context, Lord Krishna tells Arjuna:

"Thou grievest for those for whom thou should not grieve for, and yet thou speakest words about wisdom. Wise men do not grieve for the dead or for the living."

The Gita stresses the point that there should be no place for grief, either in case of death or in other circumstances. The message of the Gita is very loud and clear — why grieve over death of the perishable body when the real self in the soul, which is the master, does not die.

The principal character of life is the individual self or the soul which never dies. It is the external frame or the physical body which perishes.

The Gita treats the phenomenon of death, as follows :

Verse 22 – Chapter II
"Just as a person casts off worn out garment and puts on others that are new even so does the embodied soul casts off worn-out bodies and takes on those that are new."

After death, the soul gets a new body. Thus death is only a transformation to another life which continues on and on. In real life, this may not seem as simple and easy to understand but one must perceive and comprehend the real significance of death, as indicated in the Gita. Life may be compared to a play in a theatre. An individual plays his role as assigned in life and then one day makes his exit from the worldly scene.

Death becomes a doorway to another life, as the soul takes on another body.

The Gita considers the phenomenon of death from some other angles as well, as may be seen from the following verses :

Verse 13 – Chapter II
"As the soul passes in the body through childhood, youth and age, even so is its taking on of another body."

Thus death is merely another stage in the journey of soul through time. This is a normal and natural happening and one need not be perplexed when it happens.

Verse 27 – Chapter II
"To the one that is born death is certain and certain is birth for the one that has died. Therefore for what is unavoidable, thou should not grieve."

Evidently one should not grieve over what is unavoidable.

Let us now examine the instances of grief on occasions other than death. One may grieve in other cases such as, disease, loss of wealth and property, failure and defeat, dishonour, personal jealousy and rivalry and bad behaviour faced in everyday life. Cases of this type may be multiplied. In short, grief happens due to unfavourable circumstances which had already taken place or are still in the process of happening or are likely to happen. In all these cases. one should try his utmost to remove the obstacles, to the extent possible, and avoid the negative emotions of grief and dejections or depression. One must face the situation as it comes and act accordingly and not give in to despair and grief as these tendencies are unbecoming of a human being. One must face, observe, and analyse an adverse situation and act wisely and bravely. One must realise the fact that simply grieving will not help, so why grieve? Some soul searching and positive thinking are required to ward off grief in such cases. Firm faith in God and performance of one's duty without attachment, are very helpful to keep grief at bay.

As human beings fail to perceive and recognise the pure and indestructible self in them and are deluded and conditioned by their body, mind and intellect ego-centric combination, they suffer from grief and despair. It is only when they rediscover themselves as the pure soul or the eternal spirit and tear apart the veil of temporary and delusory relationship with the body that they will shun all grief and sorrows of existence. When a person understands this reality, there is no cause for grief either for the dead or for the living. The Gita says that a person who remains unagitated in such adverse happenings is truly wise.

Pleasure and Pain

Human life consists of pleasant and unpleasant experiences. While pleasant experiences give pleasure, unpleasant ones lead to pain. Thus pleasure and pain are like two sides of the same coin.

Where there is pleasure, there is bound to be pain also, sooner or later. Sometimes pleasure leads to pain and there may be pleasure after pain.

The *Gita* explains the cause and nature of these and also gives instructions to deal with them; as indicated in *Verse 14* of *Chapter II*, quoted below :

> "*Contacts with other objects give rise to cold and heat, pleasure and pain. These come and go and do not last for ever, learn to endure these.*"

Our joys and sorrows, pleasant and unpleasant experiences arise out of our various activities in life. These activities take place when we come in contact with the external world either in thought or in action, at home or outside.

Thus, our life itself provides opportunities for pleasure and pain. So long as we live we have to face both these situations. Pleasure and pain are therefore unavoidable. The Gita tells us how to deal with these happenings. The ultimate solution of this is in the last sentence which says, 'Learn to Endure'. There is no option but to endure. We must therefore, learn how to face these situations with calm and composure and bear them with serenity of mind, knowing that these situations are bound to pass away.

Verse 15 of *Chapter II* elucidates this futher, as follows :

"The man who is not troubled by these, who remains the same in pain and pleasure is wise and makes himself fit for eternal life."

We should meet these situations with the evenness of mind. In our moments of pleasure and happiness, we need not jump with abnormal ostentatious expressions of joy.

Similarly in moments of pain and grief, one should not feel utterly miserable and aggrieved or disturbed. Equanimity must be maintained in both cases, which may not be easy in real life situations, a correct understanding and constant practice of endurance will be helpful.

Let us now consider some examples from everyday life. We are happy and joyful at the birth of a child, on marriage in the family, success in examination or in some other event, on getting a job or promotion in career, acquisition of wealth and property and some other cases of material gain, profit or success. It is natural to feel happy in these pleasant situations, but where is the need to show over-exuberance, gaiety, over-indulgence, pomp and show? We all know how much time and money is actually wasted in these events. It is desirable to avoid such wastage.

Similarly our moments of pain may arise from physical discomfort, disease, material loss, failure, non-fulfilment of desires, abuse and dishonour and finally from death of a close friend or relative etc. Such happenings in everyday life have to the viewed as exigencies of life, accepted and endured with patience and determination. While one should make every effort to avoid painful situations and try to take all possible precautions for safety, the unavoidable has to be endured. It should always be borne in mind that there is no obligation to be over-joyed in success or to feel utterly miserable in failure.

One must face and go along with the current of whatever happens in life. The keyword is 'Endure'. The struggle of life has to be sustained through pleasure and pain, victory or defeat, success or failure, joy or sorrow, honour or dishonour, health and disease, wealth and poverty and other ups and downs alike, in a spirit of equal-mindedness. Life shall then be at peace and purposeful.

❏❏

Yoga as Defined in The Gita

The Gita has been described as the scripture of Yoga. It gives a comprehensive exposition of yoga, flexible and many-sided. The emphasis is on yoga, an inner discipline which leads to the liberation of the soul, which is the highest goal of life. The subject matter has been dealt in different ways, depicting different paths, leading to the same goal.

The first mention of yoga in the Gita is found in *Verse 39* of **Chapter II**, in which Lord Krishna tells Arjuna:

> "This is the wisdom of Sankhya given to thee. Listen now to the wisdom of yoga. If your intelligence accepts it, thou shall cast away the bondage of works."

The above verse mentions Sankhya and Yoga. The earlier verses explains the reality of immortal soul, the perishable body, different stages through which the soul passes, the inevitable death and re-birth, grief, pleasure and pain etc. This analytical study of the human life represents the wisdom of Sankhya.

Having imparted the wisdom of Sankhya to Arjuna, Lord Krishna then dwells on the wisdom of Yoga. As indicated in the subsequent verses, yoga here means Karma Yoga. In the sanskrit-text of *Verse 39* of **Chapter II**, the word Budhi Yoga has been mentioned. It implies action with true understanding. It stands for the performance of one's duty with right understanding.

The first clear definition of Yoga in the Gita is found in **Verse 48** of **Chapter II** as follows:

"Fixed in Yoga, do thy work, abandoning attachment, with an even mind in success and failure, for evenness of mind is called Yoga."

Thus yoga has been defined as evenness of mind. It is a state of inner poise, self-mastery and perfect serenity. One must perform actions, without attachment and without concern for fruits of actions.

The role of intelligence in the performance of action is also evident from **Verse 49** of **Chapter II**, as follows:

"Far inferior indeed is mere action to the discipline of intelligence. Seek refuge in intelligence. Pitiful are there who seek for the fruits of their actions."

The discipline of intelligene requires discrimination of right and wrong. A person who has right understanding will perform right actions. The Gita further mentions that the state of yoga (*samadhi*) is achieved when intelligence becomes unshaken and stable.

This verse indicates that perfection in yoga leads to the highest purity which comes from wisdom.

In **Verse 41** of **Chapter IV**, the relationship between the spirit of renunciation attained through yoga, wisdom and self-discipline are indicated, as follows:

"Works do not bind him who has renounced all works by yoga, who has destroyed all doubt by wisdom and who ever possesses his soul."

The above verse implies that all bondage and all doubts are removed through yoga.

Verse 6 of **Chapter V** indicates that an earnest practitioner of yoga achieves God-realisation and the spirit of renounciation can not be attained without yoga.

Verses 21, 23 and *24* of *Chapter V* briefly mention benefits resulting from yoga. Those who have attained yoga are no longer attached to external objects, can control desires and anger and enjoy divine bliss.

Chapter VI of the Gita deals with yoga quite extensively. The whole Chapter is replete with references to yoga, as indicated below :

Verse 2 – Chapter VI

"What they call renunciation, that know to be disciplined activity, for no one becomes a yogi who has not renounced selfish motives."

Disciplined activity without seeking its fruit brings about an inward attitude of remunciation and the same is equated with yoga.

In *Verse 50* of *Chapter II*, yoga has been described as skill in action, as follows :

"One who has fixed his understanding in the Divine, casts away both good and evil, even here in this life. Therefore strive for yoga, Yoga is skill in action."

Such a skill is acquired only when a person works at the level of intelligence while his mind rests in God. In such a state, he is liberated from the bondage of both good and bad actions.

In *Verse 3* of *Chapter III*, there is mention of Gyan Yoga (Path of knowledge) and Karma Yoga (path of Action). We will deal with these, in detail, in separate chapters.

In *Verses 1 to 4* of *Chapter IV*, yoga has been mentioned as ancient knowledge handed down from one sage to another since ancient times, although it was lost to the world for a long time till Lord Krishna again declared this knowledge to Arjuna.

In *Verse 27* of the same chapter, there is again mention of yoga of self-control kindled by knowledge. In other words self-control which results from true knowledge may be described as yoga.

It may be relevant to quote *Verse 38* of *Chapter IV*, as follows :

"There is nothing on earth equal in purity to wisdom. He who becomes perfected by yoga finds this of himself, in himself, in course of time."

Several verses in this chapter indicate the qualities which are essential ingredients of yoga practice. These include self-control, equal mindedness, true renunciation, non-attachment to external objects and happenings, serenity, freedom from desires. In yoga, there is paramount emphasis on self-control or self-discipline. A disciplined mind is liberated from all desires and this is a pre-requisite for yoga.

Verses 18-21 of *Chapter VI* mention the consequeness of having attained the state of yoga. The final stage is supreme delight *(ananda)*. Yoga is the stage of the greatest gain, free from pain, as mentioned in *Verses 22* and *23*, as follows :

Verse 22 – Chapter VI

"That, on gaining which there is no greater gain beyond it. Wherein established, he is not shaken even by the heaviest sorrow."

Verse 23 – Chapter VI

"Let that be known by the name of yoga, this disconnection from pain. This yoga should be practised with determination, with heart undismayed."

Thus yoga may be described as the culmination of human spiritual endeavour. The Gita describes yoga in different ways. It is the greatest gain; complete liberation from pain; state of complete rest and concentration, supreme happiness and infinite bliss. This is the supreme goal of life.

Verse 32 of *Chapter VI* mentions the state of a perfect yogi, as follows :

"He who sees with equality everything, in the image of his own self, whether in pleasure or in pain, he is considered a perfect yogi."

The state of perfection of a yogi is again described in *Verse 2* of *Chapter XII,* as follows :

"Those who fixing their minds on Me worship Me, ever earnest and possessed of supreme faith — them do I consider most perfect in yoga."

The Gita is full of numerous references to yoga. However, the subject is specifically dealt with under three main forms of yoga which are, Karma Yoga (Path of action), Gyan Yoga (Path of knowledge) and Bhakti Yoga (path of devotion). These three forms of yoga are dealt with in separate chapters of this book.

❏❏

Karma Yoga (Path of Action)

Chapter III of the Gita deals with this subject, in detail Life is full of action and we are bound by the results of our actions or *Karma*. According to this law of nature, every action has its reaction and thus is a source of bondage. Let us see what the Gita says in the following *Verses*:

Verse 9 – Chapter III

"Not by abstention of work does a man attain freedom from actions; nor by mere renunciation does he attain to his perfection."

Verse 5 – Chapter III

"For no one can remain ever for a moment without doing work; every one is made to act helplessly by the impulses born of nature."

These verses emphasise the role of action in life. Action is unavoidable in life. Although action leads to bondage yet mere abstention from action or renunciation does not lead to emancipation.

Our life is like a battlefield for action and *Verse* 38 of *Chapter II* tells us how to act in this battle, as quoted below:

Verse 38 – Chapter II

"Treating alike, pleasure and pain, gain and loss, victory and defeat, get ready for battle. Thus thou shall not incur sin."

According to the Gita, the battle of life has to be fought with equal-mindedness in all situations, without getting disturbed in emotional ups and downs.

Action Performed in this Spirit is Karma Yoga

The idea contained in *verse 38* quoted above is further developed in *Verse 48* of *Chapter II*, as follows:

Verse 48 – Chapter II

"Fixed in yoga, do thy work, abandoning attachment, with an even mind in success or failure, for evenness of mind is called yoga."

This verse fortifies the earlier idea of performing action with even mind and adds the condition of non-attachment.

Verse 47 of **Chapter II**, which is one of the most famous verses of the Gita, contains the essential principle of Karma Yoga. This verse is as follows:

"To action you have a right and never at all to its fruits, but not the fruits of action be thy motive; neither let there be in thou any attachment to in action."

When we do something, the act of doing is within our reach but the result is beyond our control as it also depends upon some extraneous factors as well, besides our efforts. Again the fruits of action may or may not be according to our expectations.

However it does not mean that we should not perform action or make no efforts on the plea that results are beyond us. We shall deal with this verse in detail, in a separate essay (*Nishkam Karma*).

The Gita also lays stress on understanding (intelligence) while performing action. Thus action should be performed with understanding and renouncing their fruits, free from like and dislike and with the thought of God within. The relevant verses from the Gita are quoted below:

Verse 50 - Chapter II

"One who has yoked his intelligence with the Divine, casts away both good and evil. Therefore strive for yoga. Yoga is skill inaction."

Verse 51 - Chapter II

"The wise who have united their intelligence with the Divine, renouncing the fruits of action and free from the bonds of birth, reach the sorrowless state."

The purity of spirit achieved by performing action in the manner indicated above will lead to grace of God. The same idea is further developed in *Verses 57* and *58* of *Chapter XVIII*, as follows:

Verse 57 - Chapter XVIII

"Surrendering in thought all actions to Me, regarding Me as the supreme and resorting to steadfastness in understanding fix thy thought constantly on Me."

Verse 58 - Chapter XVIII

"Fixing thy thought on Me, you shall by My grace cross over all difficulties, but if from self-conceit, you will not listen, you shall perish."

In the light of above and earlier verses quoted above, all actions should be performed with full understanding and constant thought of God without any sense of egotism.

While seeds of Karma Yoga were sown in *Chapter II*, it is in *Chapter III* that this concept is further elucidated in the following manner:

Verse 3 - Chapter III

"In this world, a two-fold way of life has been taught by Me, the path of knowledge for men of contemplation and that of works for men of action."

As observed in the real world, human beings may be broadly classified into following two types:
  i) Those whose mental disposition is towards action or worldly pursuits, and
  ii) Those who have a tendency to explore inner self.

The two paths mentioned in the above verse are equally efficient means for liberation but are intended for two different types of individuals. However, the two categories of individuals mentioned here are not exclusive but complimentary. The dividing factor is the predominance of a particular tendency in any individual who may not be a wholly man of action or of knowledge. Thus, if in an indivudual, the tendency for action is stronger, he or she should follow the path of action or Karma Yoga. The path of knowledge or Gyan Yoga is suitable for those who are more inclined towards contemplations of inner self. However, it does not mean that these paths are opposed to each other. A man of knowledge can not remain without action. Even modes like resting, thinking, sitting in silence etc. are all actions, Even not doing anything is also action. Mere maintenance of the body involves action. God is always engaged in action, as stated in the following verse:

Verse 22 – Chapter III

Lord Krishna tells Arjuna :

"There is not for me, any work in the three worlds which has to be done nor anything to be obtained which has not been obtained, yet I am engaged in action."

As such no one is free from action or Karma. Such is the role of action in life that it is not possible for any one to abstain from it. Karma or action follows a person like a shadow. It is also not desirable to stop working. The Gita teaches performance of action and does not support cessation of work. While performing action, inner restraint by the mind over the senses is essential. Mere senses outward control of organs of action while the mind continues to brood over the objects of sense, shows false conduct, as indicated in the verse quoted below:

Verse 6 – Chapter III

"He who restrains his organs of action but continues in his mind to brood over the objects of sense, he is deluded and is a hypocrite."

In *Verse 8* of *Chapter III*, the Gita lays stress on doing one's duty, as follows:

"Do thy allotted work, for action is better than inaction; even the maintenance of thy physical life can not be effected without action."

In everyday life, one has to perform certain actions, as obligatory duties, such as running of household, working for livelihood, maintenance of the body etc. These actions can not be abandoned. Thus action has to performed as a moral obligation or a physical necessity in order to contribute to the harmonious and smooth running of the cosmic mechanism.

A person who does not do so lives, in vain, as stated in *Verse 16* of *Chapter III*, as follows:

"He who does not in this world, help to turn the wheel thus set in motion, is evil in his nature, sensual in his delight and he lives in vain."

Of all the different paths of yoga described in the Gita. Karma Yoga, or the path of action, seems more suited to the householder, as every householder has to perform action in the form of obligatory duties, on a regular basis. Karma Yoga, which, in brief, is the path of right action, without attachment to its fruits, has greater role to play in the lives of vast majority. Keeping its important and essential role in view, and on the basis of various verses in the Gita, the main teachings in this regard, are summarised below:

i) All actions should be performed, with inner restraint of the mind over the senses.

ii) Action, as a matter of duty, should be performed in a spirit of sacrifice for the Divine and without egotism. The performance of one's obligatory duty in a detached manner, is the highest offering or sacrifice.

iii) All normal activities should be carried on without being obsessed by desire, but absorbed in the thought of the Supreme. Such an attitude will guide an individual towards the path of righteousness.

iv) Action should be performed with true understanding. Action and knowledge should go together. It is said that action without knowledge is blind and knowledge without action is lame.

v) All actions should be performed with an attitude of non-attachment.

vi) Action should be performed without concern for its fruits. Always feel pleasure in doing your duty without thought of impending result. Work should be done for its own sake and with an even mind, undisturbed by its consequences.

vii) One should understand one's physical and mental capabilities which determine our nature and perform action accordingly.

This is, in brief, the path of action or Karma Yoga, which should help an individual to attain the purity of mind which leads to the highest goal of life.

Nishkam Karma (Selfless Action)

"To action alone thou has a right and never, at all, to its fruits, let not fruits of action be thy motive, neither let there be any attachment to in action.

Verse 47 – Chapter II

The above famous often quoted verse of the Gita lays down the essential basic principle which should govern all our actions in everyday life. The core message is – Work without concern for the result or fruit of action.

The Gita tells us that our performance of actions should not be influenced by any thought of impending result. In other words, we should not manoeuvre our action in order to produce a result desired by our selfish motives. Normally, the reverse happens in real life. We often think more about fruits and perform action in such a way as would bring about the desired result. In this process, we ignore even the moral values. According to the Gita, work should be performed for its own sake, with whole-hearted attention, unaffected by any thought of success or failure, profit or loss, honour or dishonour, fame or loss of fame etc. Thus while doing our duty, any such extraneous considerations should not interfere. Success and failure do not depend on individual efforts alone, but on other factors, as well. Our role is to act to the best of our ability and not to worry unnecessarily about results.

The above verse gives the *moolmantra* of selfless action or *Nishkam Karma*. Literally speaking, this verse means you have a right to action but not to its fruits. It does not mean that your action will not produce any result. What is implied is that while you are required to perform action, in any given situation, you may or may not get result according to your wishes or expectations. Consequently, our performance should not be attuned to our expectations of results of our actions. It also implies that our expectations should not influence our performance.

It is not possible to put forth best efforts if one is constantly worried as to what will happen if the results do not happen as expected or desired. Our desires or expectations may not be realistic. Therefore in the performance of our actions, we must try our utmost and leave the result to God and accept it without complaint or grumbling.

Verse 48 of **Chapter II** is very appropriate in this regard and the same is quoted below :

"Fixed in yoga, do thy work, abandoning attachment, with an even mind in success and failure, for evenness of mind is called yoga."

This is the essence of 'Nishkam Karma' which should govern all actions in life.

Gyan Yoga (Path of Knowledge)

True knowledge which leads to the experience of the ultimate reality is wisdom pure and transcendent, different from theoretical knowledge or information. The path of knowledge or Gyan Yoga is the intellectual path to perfection. Spiritual vision is necessary for knowing the reality of the Ultimate Truth.

Ignorance is the cause of desires which leads to human bendage. So long as ignorance persists, the final goal of liberation of the soul can not be achieved. Ignorance must, therefore, be removed. True knowledge is the means to remove ignorance. It is the light which illumines the soul and gives Divine experience. To achieve this, first of all, the soul has to be cleansed of all accompanying impurities of human blemishes of anger, fear, greed, attachment, false pride, and all selfish desires.

The Gita provides the theory of this knowledge. It gives the knowledge of the Supreme, the individual self and nature. It explains the distinction between the individual self and the body. It indicates the cause of pleasure and pain. It tells us how we can have even mind, by uniting our intelligence with the Divine, and by renouncing the fruits of our actions. It also tells us about the immortality of the spirit and the meaning of existence. It shows the way that leads to stable intelligence through contentment and by putting away all the desires of the mind.

Gyan Yoga is the product of mind and intelligence of an individual, while his thoughts rest in God. Here the right understanding becomes the main instrument of spiritual realisation by lifting the individual consciousness to the supreme consciousness. The way of knowledge lies through unflinching faith, constant devotion and worship. Let us see how Gita declares this in the following Verses:

Verse 10 – Chapter X

"To those who are constantly devoted and worship Me with love, I grant the concentration of understanding by which they come into Me."

Verse 11 – Chapter X

"Out of compassion for these same ones, remaining within My own true state, I destroy the darkness of ignorance by the shining lamp of wisdom."

Thus constant devotion, worship and love of God are necessary to acquire wisdom which of course comes with the grace of God and not merely by human efforts. However, one has to grow to the final phase through mental control and self-discipline. The fire of passion, desire and attachment must be extinguished. One must control the senses but this is not to be achieved through suppression but through regular practice and with a spirit of sacrifice. Every form of self-control, where one sacrifices enjoyment of senses, is a means to attain knowledge.

In *Verse* 34 of *Chapter IV*, the Gita tells the way how knowledge can be actually gained through learning process and with the help of the wise, as indicated below:

Verse 34 – Chapter IV

"Learn that by humble reverence, by inquiry and by service. The men of wisdom who have seen the truth will instruct thee in knowledge."

The above *Verse* shows the necessity of a true and competent guide who himself has attained true knowledge.

In *Verses 7 to 10* of *Chapter XIII*, several moral virtues, which form ingredients of knowledge are mentioned. The practice of these virtues lead to the final insight, as concluded in *Verse 11*, quoted below:

Verse 11 – Chapter XIII

"Constancy in the knowledge of the spirit, insight into the end of the knowledge of Truth – this is declared to be true knowledge and all that is different from it is non-knowledge."

It is clear from above that merely theoretical learning is not enough to acquire true knowledge which essentially includes practice of all moral virtues.

When knowledge is gained, all ignorance is removed and what was earlier obscure becomes clear. A person who has attained knowledge has complete control over his desires and his mind rests in God. There is nothing on earth equal in purity to true knowledge, as stated in **Verse 38** of **Chapter IV**:

"There is nothing on earth equal in purity to wisdom. He who becomes perfected by yoga finds this of himself, in his self, in course of time."

❏❏

Bhakti Yoga (Path of Devotion)

"By unswerving devotion to Me. O! Arjuna, I can be thus known, truly seen and entered into."

Verse 54 – Chapter XI

The above verse tells us that the Supreme can be attained through devotion. There are other verses in the Gita which emphasise the role of devotion for God-realisation, some of which are quoted below:

Verse 55 – Chapter XI

"He who does work for Me, he who looks upon Me as his goal, he who worships Me, free from attachment, he who is free from enmity to all creatures, he goes to Me."

Verse 6 – Chapter XII

"But those, who, laying all their actions on Me, intent on Me, worship, meditating on me, with unswerving devotion."

All these verses and some others, as well, clearly indicate how path of devotion or Bhakti Yoga can lead to perfection and achieve the highest goal. Devotion does not exclude action but action has to be performed without attachment and as a sacrifice to God. Devotion thus includes action without attachment, friendliness to all, compassion and freedom from enmity and egoism and full understanding which dwells on the Supreme. It implies worship of God with complete faith.

Devotion is the path of love which is neither merely physical attention nor intellectual appreciation. It is love not for things material but love for a higher ideal. It is love at the level of the Supreme. It is not superficial and emanates from the heart. Devotion to God is the highest and the purest form of love. Love in the ordinary sense may be fascination or attraction for a person or one object etc. Such love is limited and temporary. We may call it attachment.

Devotion or Bhakti is spontaneous and for a higher cause. Simply going to a temple or a place of worship or performing some specific religious rites on certain occasions is not necessarily devotion. Devotion involves intense love and longing, unselfish love without asking for anything and without sensual enjoyment.

There are several verses in *Chapter XII* of the Gita which describe the qualities of a true devotee. Some of these verses are quoted as follows :

Verse 13 – Chapter XII

"He who has no ill will to any being, who is friendly and compassionate, free from egoism and self sense, even-minded in pain and pleasure and patient."

Verse 14 – Chapter XII

"The yogi who is ever content, self-controlled, unshakable in determination, with mind and understanding given up to Me - he My devotee is dear to Me."

Verse 15 – Chapter XII

"He from whom the world does not turn away and who does not shrink from the world and also is free from anger, fear and agitation, he too is dear to me."

There are other verses too, which mention several other qualities. Thus in the path of devotion or Bhakti Yoga, there is great emphasis on qualities rather than mere performance of some religious rituals. Broadly speaking, these qualities are moral values, which include, love, humility, mercy, gentleness, even-mindedness, self-restraint, contentment, firm determination; absence of egoism, anger, fear and attachment and some more. The service of humanity is also an essential aspect of devotion.

Constant remembrance of God with full faith, contemptation of his attributes, singing his praises, performing actions without attachment, in the spirit of service to God and practice of qualities mentioned above in real conduct and behaviour are part of discipline of devotion.

According to the Gita, the worship of God may be practised in two ways :

(1) Worship of the absolute, impersonal God

(2) Worship of a personal God, a material being

Both types of worship lead to the same goal. However, as pointed out in *Verse 5* of *Chapter XII* of the Gita, it may be more difficult to realise the formless Supreme because identification with the un-manifest, the formless, is not easy. This verse is quoted as follows :

Verse 5 – Chapter XII

"The difficulty of those whose thoughts are set on the unmanifested is greater for the goal of the unmanifested is hard to reach."

The Gita tells us that those who worship God with supreme faith and earnestness are the most perfect in yoga. This view is expressed in **Verse 2** of **Chapter XII**, as follows :

"Those who fixing their mind on Me worship Me ever earnest and endowed with supreme faith, them I consider most perfect in yoga."

Earnestness and unflinching faith are the main ingredients of true devotion. The true devotee meditates on God with true love and all his actions are God-oriented. All his thoughts are fixed on HIM. Devotion involves complete surrender to the Supreme. The path of devotion takes its stand upon the love and emotions of a person and turns these towards God. Individual ego is destroyed by the intensity of love of God. If does not take into account the reflection and reasoning of the mind and makes full use of love and adoration of the Divine. It is the yearning of the eager heart and seeks divine fulfilment of the emotional being of a person. To conclude, the attention of the readers may be invited to the two, significant verses of the Gita as follows :

Verse 34 – Chapter IX

"On Me, fix thy mind, to Me be devoted; worship Me, rever Me; thus having disciplined thyself, with Me as thy goal, to Me shalt thou come."

Verse 65 – Chapter XVIII

"Fix thy mind on Me; be devoted to Me; sacrifice to Me, prostrate thyself before Me; so shalt thou come to Me. I promise thee truly, for thou art dear to Me."

❑❑

Synthesis of Yoga

The Gita describes three separate paths of Yoga which may be followed individually by persons of different temperaments. However, it does not mean that a single particular path has to be pursued rigidly by a certain individual. The practice of a particular path by an individual depends, by and large, upon the nature of the practitioner. In actual practice, these paths can not be practised in isolation, but these have to be intertwined to achieve the final goal.

To start with, one has to practise a particular path, influenced by his innate temperament. For instance, an action-oriented person should follow the path of action or Karma Yoga. But while doing so, he needs knowledge in order to discriminate between right and wrong action. Besides, he also needs to practise devotion, in some form or the other. Similarly, a man of knowledge or devotion has to perform action, as no one can remain without action. There is a saying that action without knowledge is blind and knowledge without action is lame. Either can not succeed without the help of the other. The purity acquired through right action and right knowledge would lead to devotion. Similarly, a person of sincere devotion acquires purity and right knowledge and therefore would perform right actions. Thus right knowledge, right action and true devotion can not be separated and all these three paths have to be fused together in spiritual practice. Thus the triple path of yoga works together to form a single movement of self-offering to the Supreme. The Gita propounds a magnificient synthesis of various strands of spirituality and paves the way for a harmonious development of human personality towards perfection. Action, Knowledge and Devotion are blended together for the divine fulfilment of man.

The correct understanding of the fundamentals of creation (*i.e.* God, Nature and Soul), performance of right actions, without concern for their fruits, and complete reverence and surrender to God — all these ingredients combine together to achieve self-realisation or God-realisation, which is the ultimate goal of life.

❏❏

Three Types of Gunas

In *Verse 5* of *Chapter XIV*, the Gita mentions about the three type of *Gunas* (modes) as follows :

"*The three gunas (modes), sattava (goodness), Rajas (passion), Tamas (dullness), born of nature bind down in the body, the imperishable dweller (soul) of the body.*"

The above three gunas are the basis of all substances. All human activities are influenced by these gunas. The word guna, implies the attitude or tendency or the condition in which the mind functions. These gunas are inherent in all beings in varying degrees and thus these determine their activities and character. The soul in the individual comes under the influence of these gunas which are the three constituents of nature. Nobody is free from these gunas although in each being, one or the other gunas may predominate.

The above three gunas may be briefly described as follows :

Sattava (Goodness)

It reflects the light of consciousness and represents purity and luminosity. It lights up the intellect and is free from evil tendencies. When this guna dominates, it brings knowledge and happiness in the life of an individual. It represents goodness and has inspiring and creative influence on the mind. The Satvik people like pure foods which help to increase vitality, joy and cheerfulness. Satvik foods are palatable, pleasant and non-violent. The fruits of satvik action are pure, good and pleasant. After death satvik people are reborn at higher levels of mankind.

Rajas (Passion)

It is in the nature of passion and is born out of attachment and desire. Passions, which are salient features of a Rajsik individual, express themselves in different desires, emotions, feelings. This mode has outward movement and binds the soul with actions connected with the external world. When Rajas is dominant in a person, selfish motives and actions, greed, restlessness, craving for pleasures are generated. It prompts material activity and produces desires for acquisition of possessions and ever looks for situations which yield to temporary pleasures and continuous attachment with them. Such an individual is ever engaged in earning and spending, procuring and preserving and always desiring for more and more. He is always agitated and entangled in the joys of his success and displeased at his failures. The fruits of Rajsik actions are miserable. Rajsik people, after death, are re-born as men of selfish motives and activities.

Tamas (Dullness)

This guna creates delusion and is source of ignorance. It binds the soul with indulgence, lethargy and sleep and leads to dullness. When tamas is dominant in a person, he loses discrimination of wrong and right. He becomes a slave of its lower nature and indolence. There is absence of noble thoughts and actions.

The fruits of Tamsik actions are ignorance. Such people, after death, sink to the lowest levels of existence.

As mentioned earlier, these gunas are present in beings in different degrees. Thus individuals are Satvik, Rajsik, Tamsik, on the basis of the particular guna which prevails or is predominant. When Sattav is predominant, knowledge, peace and discernment rule the mind. When Rajas prevails greed, selfishness and desires overcome and when Tamas dominates, indolence, delusion and ignorance rule. In general, Sattav is for goodness, Rajas is for passions and Tamas is for dullness and ignorance.

When the soul in the individual comes under the influence of gunas, it forgets its real self and uses body, mind and senses for temporary satisfaction and pleasures which are binding. When the soul rises above the three modes of nature, it gets liberated and attains the Supreme, as indicated in the following Verse :

Verse 20 – Chapter XIV

"When the embodied soul rises above these three modes of nature, it is freed from birth, death, old age and pain and attains life eternal."

Thus after having become aware of three gunas, a wise person shall surely try to inculcate Satvik gunas in his life. By means of Sattava, one can overcome ill effects of Rajas and Tamas. By developing the element of sattva gradually through long practice, one has to try to get beyond all gunas and achieve the perfect stage of eternal life.

❑❑

Three-fold Classification

Based on three gunas (or modes of nature) the Gita in *Chapter XVII* and *XVIII* classifies various phenomena and activities concerning human life. These are briefly described below:

1. Faith

Faith is the first item mentioned in the Gita. It is not mere acceptance of a belief. It is the inner urge or the impelling fire within, which enables an individual to strive for self-realisation, or act in a given direction.

A person has faith according to his inherent nature. Human beings have three kinds of faith based on three gunas. The personality of an individual is determined by the faith or influence under which it functions.

The Satvik or pure persons worship God, the Rajsik or the passionate ones worship demi-gods or deities and the Tamsik or the dull persons worship spirits and ghosts.

In real life, Satvik persons are serene and are engaged in divine and noble pursuits. Persons of Rajsik temperament are ambitious, restless and are fond of propitiating demi-gods. The Tamsik seek their satisfaction in vicious powers, and dead elements.

2. Food

Foods which promote life, purity, health and strength and are sweet, soft, nourishing and savoury are Satvik foods.

Foods which are sour, salty, exceedingly hot and pungent are Rajsik.

Foods which are stale, stinking, and unclean are tamsik.

3. Charity

The charity given as a matter of duty and without expectation of return, to the right and deserving person, at the right time and place is Satvik.

The charity given with the expectation of a return or some gain or with reluctance or under compulsion is Rajsik.

The charity given to a wrong, undeserving person, at wrong time and place or in hate and anger is Tamsik.

4. Knowledge

True knowledge that leads to God and promotes righteousness is Satvik. Through such knowledge, one God is observed in all existence.

The knowledge that leads to divisions and separateness in different creatures is Rajsik.

The knowledge that leads to ignorance and unreality is Tamsik.

5. Action

An obligatary action performed writhout attachment and without expectation of any reward is Satvik.

Action perfomed under strain and impelled by selfishness and for the gratification of desires is Rajsik.

Action performed out of ignorance and without any regard for consequences and humam capacity is Tamsik.

6. Understanding

The understanding which discriminates between right and wrong, desirable and undesirable is Satvik.

That which produces wrong impression and is misleading is Rajsik.

That which holds wrong as right and sees all things in a perverted way (contrary to the reality) is Tamsik.

7. Steadiness

Steadiness which is unwavering and controls mind, life breath and senses is Satvik.

That by which one performs action, desiring fruits, pleasure and wealth is Rajsik.

That which induces sleep, fear, grief, depression and arrogance is Tamsik.

8. Sacrifice

Sacrifice which is performed as a matter of duty and without expectation of any reward is Satvik.

Sacrifice offered with expectation of reward or for ostentatious parpose is Rajsik.

Sacrifice offered without faith and in disregard of righteousness is Tamsik.

9. Penance

Penance performed with faith and without expectation of rewards is Satvik. These include celibacy, purity, non-violence, uprightness. and practice of truth.

Penance peformed for the sake of show or for gaining fame or admiration or honour is Rajsik.

Penance which is performed with foolish obstinacy, by torturing mind and body and by harming others is Tamsik.

10. Happiness

The happiness which is gained through long practice and which ends all sorrow is Satvik. Such happiness springs from clarity of understanding and is not superficial.

The happiness which results from the gratification of sensual derises is Rajsik.

Happiness arising from ignorance, sloth and negligence is Tamsik.

The above examples show how three Gunas can influence human character and activities. These gunas are born of nature and keep the individual soul in bondage. So long as the soul remains in bondage, human beings will continue to experience pleasure and pain on the basis of these gunas. Among these, the Satvik gunas are the most desirable. However, mere acquisition of Satvik gunas is not the ultimate stage of human development. This stage can act as a stepping stone for achieving the ultimate goal of life. By constant practice and restraint, one can transcend the satvik stage and achieve the final stage of redemption of the soul.

❏❏

Four-fold Order of Society

All human beings are governed by the three modes (qualities) of nature. These modes are *Sattava* (goodness) *Rajas* (passion) and *Tamas* (dullness).

Verse 40 – Chapter XVIII

There is no being on earth or again in heaven, among the gods, who is totally liberated from the three qualities (modes) born of nature.

Verse 5 – Chapter XIV

The three modes (gunas) sattava (goodness), rajas (passion) and tamas (dullness), born of nature build the imperishable soul to the body.

Verse 41 – Chapter XVIII

The activities of Brahmins, the Kshatriyas, the Vaishyas and the Shudras has been divided in accordance with the qualities of their nature.

Individuals differ from one another, because of the presence of these three gunas in different proportions in them. Accordingly they have different types of character and behaviour. Based on the presence of these qualities in different individuals, the Gita classifies the entire society into four types. This classification is not determined by their birth in a particular household. Colour or heredity are not the decisive factors either. This classification is based on individual characteristics and inherent attitudes by virtue of which they are fit to perform appropriate function in the society. It is emphasised that caste, based on birth in a particular family, is not at all the basis to categorise these classes, as has become the norm in the present day society. The existing classification of Brahmins, Kshatriya, Vaishya and Shudras has resulted from selfish manoeuvering of the vested interests, where parents, because of various selfish and social factors did not want their progeny to lose the benefits accruing from their respective established status. Unfortunately, it has resulted into the prevailing evils of caste system which has divided the Hindu community into high caste and low caste individuals. This obnoxious and unnatural division has become the bane of present day socio-political system. This is not at all recommended or sanctioned by the Gita.

According to the Gita, the social fabric of entire humanity (and not Hindus alone) is classified into four distinct types, on the basis of various modes, gunas, or qualities inherent in respective individuals. These types are as follows :

1. Brahmins

They are persons of wisdom and knowledge. Their traits include serenity, self-restraint, purity, austerity, uprightness, forgiveness. Such individuals have firm faith in God and moral values. They are righteous people, teachers and spiritual leaders and as such can provide wise counsel and proper guidance to the ruling elite and society, in general.

2. Kshatriyas

They are those people who possess prowess, vigour, splendour, firmness, resourcefulness, generosity, boldness and leadership qualities. They are the warrior individuals, who are not afraid of battle.

3. Vaishyas

They are proficient in agriculture trade and commerce. They form the business class and farming community.

4. Shudras

They provide physical services to others.

The above four types of individuals perform different types of jobs depending upon their nature and capability, which is the consequence of their respective gunas or qualities inherent in them.

The mental and physical equipment of an individual determines the role he is fit to play in society. Accordingly, a son of a so-called Brahmin, who does not possess the mental temperament, knowledge and wisdom aquired of that type, is not fit to be called a Brahmin. So is the case with other types. But in actual practice, this is not happening. A son of a Brahmin or a Kshatriya continues to be categorised so, simply because he happens to be born of such parents. This unfair practice has resulted in the obnoxious caste system and its consequent evils and malpractices. It is both desirable and essential that religious and political leaders, social reformers and intellectuals combine together and spread the message of the Gita in this respect, in a proper perspective.

❏❏

Renunciation and Relinquishment

"The wise understand by 'renunciation' the giving up of works prompted by desire and some feel that the abandonment of the fruits of works in relinquishment."

Verse 2 – Chapter XVIII

To renounce, literally means to abandon, to give up something. Renunciation, therefore involves giving up of objects, and abandoning of work or action. As generally understood by a householder, it would imply that he should leave his household and retire to a forest or an *ashram* or become a wandering monk, called *Sanyasi* having abondoned all material possessions.

In *Verse 4* of the same Chapter, the Gita says that the relinquishment is three-fold—Satvik, Rajsik and Tamsik. According to the Gita, acts of sacrifice, charity and penance *(Tap)* are not to be given-up. These acts are to be performed, giving up attachment and desire of fruits.

If such acts are abandoned due to ignorance, then, this is a case of TAMSIK relinquishment.

If these are given up because these are painful, it is a case of RAJSIK relinquishment.

However, if a person performs duty because it has to be performed renouncing all attachment as well as their fruits then it is SATVIK relinquishment.

Thus the renunciation of any duty that should be done is not right.

Here the enphasis is not on the renunciation of action, but on the renunciation of attachment and the desire for fruits of action. The Gita does not conform to the view that all actions should be abandoned under the belief that action leads to bondage. Therefore, all obligatory duties have to be undertaken.

True renunciation is at the level of mind, which jobs are being attended to at the physical level. It means working with a detached spirit. It implies emptiness of all impurities resulting from desire, greed, anger and attachment. When the soul is rid of all these blemishes, it lives in the consciousness of the Divine and attains the beatitude of God. When the soul is no longer attached to external objects, through the mind and the senses, one finds true happiness. Thus inner Joy and peace can be achieved through renunciation, freedom from desire and non-attachment. This is a mental attitude which can be sustained amidst a worldly life, without retiring to a forest.

In *Verse 2* of *Chapter VI* renunciation is equated with disciplined activity, as follows :

> "What they call renunciation, know to be disciplined activity, for no one becomes a Yogi who has not renounced his selfish purpose."

The Gita insists not on renunciation of action but on disciplined action with renunciation of attachment and desire for fruits of action. In fact, the Gita shows preference for unselfish performance of works over renunciation of works, as stated in *Verse 2* of *Chapter V* :

> "The renunciation of works and their unselfish performance both lead to soul's salvation. But of the two, the unselfish performance of works is better than their renunciation."

The renunciation of works here involves renunciation of selfish works which lead to bondage. According to the

Gita, a true worker who works without attachment and desire for fruits of action is a true renouncer as he does his work in a detached spirit.

Let us now consider relinquishment (abandonment) or *Tyag*. Both renunciation (*sanyas*) and relinquishment (*tyag*) are inter-related disciplines. To a casual thinker both appear to be same. But relinquishment is slightly different from renunciation. While renunciation implies absence of action or absence of a desire behind an action, relinquishment implies absence of desire for the fruit of action. Renunciation is the goal to be achieved through the means of relinquishment. Both these activities involve self-denial or giving-up of something. Relinquishment or *tyag* is the real content of renunciation or *sanyas*.

❑❑

Devotees of God

"The virtuous ones who worship Me are of four kinds, the man in distress, the seeker of knowledge, the seeker of wealth and the man of wisdom."
                                      Verse 16 – Chapter VII

The above verse mentions four kinds of worshippers. Most of the worshippers ask for something–wealth, material possessions, children, success in worldly pursuits, relief from sufferings and so on. The fourth kind of devotees are rare. They are single-minded devotees whose wisdom is concentrated on the Supreme. They seek nothing material, accept whatever comes to them and submit to the Divine will, whole-heartedly. They are without selfish desires and worship God with purity of heart and complete devotion. They are close to the Divine and are most dear to HIM. Ultimately, such a devotee achieves the highest goal of life–may be in the present life or after more lives.

Persons whose minds are disturbed by mundane desires worship gods and goddesses consistent with their inherent impulses. The Gita says:

"Whatever form any devotee, with faith, wishes to worship, I make that faith steady."
                                      Verse 21 – Chapter XVII

God recognises the faith of even those who follow other gods and grants the rewards they seek. But gains achieved by these persons are of temporary nature only. God accepts the prayers of the faithful and answers them at the level at which worshippers approach Him.

In **Verses 13 to 19** of **Chapter XII** of the Gita, Lord Krishna enumerates the qualites of a True Devotee. These are brifly mentioned here :

- ❖ He is friendly and compassionate and bears no ill-will.
- ❖ He is patient and even-minded in pleasure and pain.
- ❖ He is free from false pride and egoism.
- ❖ He is contented, self-controlled, firm in resolves and fully dedicated to God.
- ❖ He does not harm others.
- ❖ He is free from envy, fear and anxiety.
- ❖ He has no expectations and is free from dependence on the outside world.
- ❖ He is skillful in action, unconcerned and untroubled.
- ❖ He is pure-hearted and has renounced fruits of all his actions.
- ❖ He neither rejoices, nor hates, nor grieves, nor desires.
- ❖ He has same attitude towards friends and foes.
- ❖ He is free from attachment and remains undisturbed in heat and cold, pleasure and pain, success or failure.
- ❖ He is restrained in speech, unaffected by blame and praise and always content.
- ❖ He has no fixed abode and has a steady mind, devoted to God.

All such devotees are dear to God but a devotee who has complete faith in God and considers Him, his supreme goal is exceedingly dear to Him. Only a spiritually oriented person can make efforts and aspire to be so!

Good and Evil Tendencies

"There are two types of beings created in the world—the divine and the demoniac..."
Verse 6 – Chapter XVI

The Gita mentions two broad types of people in the world. They represent good and evil tendencies. According to the Gita, those born with divine nature have following qualities :

- Fearlessness, purity of mind, knowledge and concentration, self-control, charity, austerity, sacrifice, study of scriptures and uprightness.
- Non-violence, truth, absence from anger, renunciation, tranquility, compassion, absence of fault-finding, freedom from greed, humility, modesty and steadiness.
- Vigour, forgiveness, fortitude, purity, absence of malice and excessive pride.

Lord Krishna mentions above distinctive qualities of a perfect divine person. In actual life, all these qualities may not be fully present even in a learned or publically adored holy person, not to speak of an ordinary person. It seems Lord Krishna has standardised a set of good qualities for which an aspirant for divine perfection should make efforts. This is an ideal to be achieved. As human beings are expected to make sincere efforts to imbibe as many of these qualities as is possible for them, during the present span of their life. Our present life is a field of action for the practice of these divine qualities. Every effort made to acquire these qualities is a step towards achieving divine perfection. This should be the aim of a true aspirant of God-realisation.

The Gita, also mentions the evil tendencies which are summed up as follows:
- Hypocrisy, arrogance, excessive pride, anger and harshness, ignorance, ostentation, excessive desires, delusion and wrong beliefs.
- Lack of understanding, lack of purity and good conduct, falsehood, cruelty in deeds, lust for wealth and possessions, obstinacy.

The above tendencies represent evil. The highest aim of the demonic is the gratification of desires—which are insatiable. They believe in the materialistic doctrine–eat, drink and be merry till you live and there is nothing beyond death. Such people fall an easy prey to all sorts of temptations in life and they do not hesitate to use even foul and wicked means to achieve their selfish aims. They have no regard for ethics and practice of moral values. Our world is full of such people and that is why there is abundance of crime, unrest, injustice and corrupt practices in all walks of life.

The Gita clearly describes distinctive tendencies which make a person divine or demoniac. However, in real life, most human beings are neither wholly divine nor wholly demonic. There may be traces of evil in a person who is generally known to be good and vice-versa. Broadly speaking, there are both good and evil tendencies in each person. It is the surfeit of either of these tendeneies which make a person good or bad.

The list of good and evil tendencies, as described in the Gita is comprehensive and self-explanatory. These can provide guidelines to a common person who will, for reasons apparant, would like to imbibe good tendencies and thus play a useful role in the society. The above list can serve a moral code of conduct for any God-loving and truly religion-oriented person. The practice of good tendencies in everyday behaviour will no doubt bring rich dividends both to the individual as well as the community around him.

Triple Gate of Hell

According to the Gita, three main evil tendencies of lust, anger and greed lead to hell. One should abandon these.

Verse 21 – Chapter XVII.

"The gateway of hell leading to the ruin of the soul is three-fold, lust, anger and greed. Therefore these three, one should abandon."

It may be pertinent to mention here that Heaven and Hell are not out of the world or imaginary places or destinations. These represent actual, real life good or miserable living situations in the existing world or the reincarnated world (*i.e.* life after death). The above three evils are the main causes of making life hell in the real world. One must, therefore, take full care to avoid these tendencies and make life heavenly on earth.

It may also be relevant here to invite readers attention to the two *Verses* of *Chapter II* of the Gita, which are quoted as follows :

Verse 62 – Chapter II

"When a man dwells in his mind on the objects of senses, attachment to them is produced. From attachment, springs desire and from desire comes anger."

When a person thinks of a sense object, again and again, he gets attached to that object. Consequently a desire to have or use that object is produced in him. Thus repetition of thought for the same object leads to desire and one longs to fulfill that desire. When desire is fulfilled once, same thoughts come again leading to same desire. When a desire is fulfilled again and again, if becomes a habit and this is how we become a slave to our desires. But desires are insatiable and one longs for more and more and this produces a vicious circle. This is how addictions to certain types of food, smoking, drinking and even drugs are produced and make life miserable. When a desire remains unfulfilled, anger is produced and the consequences of anger are indicated in the following verse :

Verse 63 – Chapter II

"From anger arises bewilderment, from bewilderment loss of memory, from loss of memory, the destruction of intelligence and from destruction of intelligence, he perishes."

This is how anger can lead to havoc. An angry person, loses balance of mind and in such a situation, he does not listen to any advice. He loses sense of discrimination and in that state comes to great harm. In everyday life we come accross several cases of disputes which lead to fatal consequences, resulting from uncontrolled anger.

The Gita, thus, clearly lays down the consequences of practising good and evil tendenceis. Those who are devoted to God, have divine qualities and follow moral codes while those who have evil tendencies violate moral codes.

In conclusion, as pointed out in the Gita, the divine qualities lead to heaven and liberation while evil tendencies lead to bondage and hell.

❏❏

The Field and Its Knower

The living organism consists of the life element and the inert matter cover through which the former functions. The life element is the spirit and the matter cover is the body. All activities take place in the body which is therefore rightly called the 'field' and the spirit is called the knower of the field. These are also mentioned as *Prakriti (Nature)* and *Purusha* (Spirit).

The spirit itself has no visible functioning except when it functions through nature or matter. All human activities are therefore an inter-play of spirit and matter or the field and the knower of the field. At the level of an individual living being, as long as the spirit remains in the body the latter has life and when the former leaves the material equipment, the body becomes dead. Thus the birth, growth, decline and death take place in the body—which is the field of action for the spirit. In the totality of the world of matter, which consists of countless 'fields' or bodies, there is One Spirit the Universal Spirit or the Supreme God who functions as the knower of all fields. The spirit which functions at the individual level is a spark of the Universal Spirit.

The knowledge of the field (body) and its knower (spirit) is regarded as true knowledge as stated in *Verse 2* of *Chapter XIII* of the Gita, and the same is quoted below :

> "Know Me as the knower of the field in all fields O, Arjuna, The knowledge of the field and its knower, do, I regard as true knowledge."

The Gita provides a precise insight into this knowledge. First the field which consists of five subtle elements ether, air, fire, water and earth, the ego, the intellect nature and five senses (sound, touch, colour, taste, and smell). Besides, desire, aversion, pleasure, pain, various parts of the body are also included in the totality of knowledge. All these are subject to change. These 24 factors constitute the field which not only has grass body, mind and intellect but also the perceptions experienced through them, emotions and thoughts. In short the entire material world is the field and the Gita calls it the body.

Next is the knowing principle—the spirit which functions as the knower of the field. This operates at two levels—at the level of individual body and at the universal level. Thus it acts as the individual soul and also as the Supreme soul. When it acts as an individual soul, it is the knower of only one field. As Supreme soul it knows all the fields *i.e.*, everything. The individual soul is dependent upon the Supreme Soul. Again the individual soul has limited power while the Supreme Soul is all powerful. The individual soul accumulates desires, deficiencies and impurity while the Supreme Soul is pure and perfect.

According to the Gita, the field which acts is constituted of nature and its spirit. They are not independent entities. We have separately mentioned in a later chapter (God and Nature) that God has two natures—lower and higher. The origin, maintenance and dissolution of the universe is caused through these. The lower nature is the cause of the field or the material world while higher nature is the experience—which at the individual level may be called as the soul and at the universal level, as the Supreme or the Universal Spirit which is the knower of all fields.

The role played by the two natures of God are apparent from the following *Verses* of *Chapter XIII* of the Gita.

Verse 19 – Chapter XIII

"Know thou that Prakriti (Nature) and Purusha (Soul) are both beginningless and know also that forms and modes are born of Prakriti (Nature)."

Verse 20 – Chapter XIII

"Nature is the cause of effect, the instrument and agent and the soul is the cause of the experience of pleasure and pain."

Verse 21 – Chapter XIII

"The soul in nature enjoys the modes born of nature and its attachment to the modes is the cause of its birth in good and evil wombs."

Verse 22 – Chapter XIII

"The Supreme spirit in the body is the witness, the supporter, the permitter and the experience."

These verses also point out the discrimination between the soul and the nature. The Gita deals with the principles of knowledge in another way also.

In *Verses 7 to 17* of *Chapter XIII* of the Gita, several moral qualities and ascetic practices are mentioned. The practice of these moral virtues leads to spiritual insight and the experience of the Supreme Reality. Mere theoretical information is not enough, it is the actual practice which matters. Therefore the knowledge includes the practice of moral qualities mentioned in the Gita. These qualities are briefly summed up below :

- Humility, which means absence of pride, absence of deceit, non-violence, patience, uprightness, service of the learned, purity of body and mind.
- Steadfastness and self-control, indifference to the objects of the senses, absence of egoism, perception of all evils of birth, death, sickness, pain, old age,

non-attachment, absence of attachment to wife, children, home, property etc. and even-mindedness in all situations, good or bad.
- Unswerving devotion to God with whole-hearted discipline, solitude and dislike for a crowd of people, constancy in the knowledge of the Spirit and insight of the Divine.

The totality of the above mentioned moral virtues and attainments is declared as true knowledge and all that is different from it is ignorance.

The aim of true knowledge is to re-discover the Supreme. This is the goal by attaining which life eternal is gained. The Gita gives an elaborate description of the Supreme, which may be briefly described, as follows:

He is without beginning.

He may be treated as non-existent, as he can not be perceived, felt or seen. At the same time, He can be declared as existent, as He is manifesting Himself through creation.

He is the Life Principle present and functioning everywhere. In this regard, it may be pertinent to quote **Verse 17** of **Chapter XIII** as follows :

"He is the light of lights, beyond all darkness. He is all knowledge, the object of knowledge and the goal of knowledge. He is seated in the hearts of all."

The Supreme can be also be described, in a series of paradoxes, as follows :
- He is devoid of senses, yet sees, hears.
- He is unattached, yet supports everything.
- He is without gunas, yet enjoys them.
- He is without and within all beings.
- He is unmoving yet moving also.
- He is far away, yet very near too.
- He is indivisible, yet seems to be divided among beings.

The Supreme which resides within all is the one and the same. He is all-pervading and supports everything. Without Him, life is impossible. He is imperishable. He is the ultimate goal to be achieved through different paths described in the Gita—paths of action, knowledge and devotion. He, who, verily sees the universal spirit in all beings, attains the supreme goal. He who perceives, with the aid of true knowledge, the difference between the field (body) and the knower of the field (the spirit), attains salvation.

❑❑

Desires

Desires act as catalytic agents for actions in life. There is hardly anyone who is free from desires. The pursuit of desire can lead to material progress and success in the world but it can also lead to destruction. The Gita deals with this topic in *Verses 62 to 63* of *Chapter II,* as follows:

Verse 62 – Chapter II

"When a man dwells in his mind on the objects of sense, attachment to them is produced. From attachment springs desire and from desire comes anger."

Verse 63 – Chapter II

"From anger, arise bewilderment and from bewilderment, loss of memory, the destruction of intelligence and from the destruction of intelligence he perishes."

As indicated in *Verse 62,* the source of desire is attachment to sense objects. When we see an object and think about it constantly, attachment is produced. The intensity of attachment produces a desire to possess or enjoy or use that object in some way or the other. A desire is, therefore, a passionate feeling born out of attachment to a sense object. Desires, in some form or shape, are constantly being produced in the mind of an individual. If one desire of a person is satisfied, the urge to satisfy another crops up.

This interplay of unending desires create a world of illusion or *mayajal* and this play of desires ends only with the end of life. It is generally observed that desires are insatiable and one desire may lead to more. In case desires are not satisfied, one is likely to get angry and anger leads to destruction of intelligence and consequent total loss. Anger results in the loss of sense of discrimination and when this happens the consequences are disastrous.

Desire is never satisfied by the enjoyment of the object of desire. Like fire to which fuel is added, the desire grows more and more with enjoyment and indulgence, as is evident from *Verse 39* of *Chapter III* of the Gita, quoted below :

Verse 39 – Chapter III

"Enveloped is wisdom, by the insatiable fire of desire, which is the constant foe of the wise."

The Gita further points out that the senses, the mind and the intelligence are overwhelmed by desire, and the soul also gets deluded. The Gita offers a solution through the control of senses, as stated in *Verse 41* of *Chapter III* quoted below :

Verse 41 – Chapter III

"Therefore, control thy senses from the beginning and slay this sinful destroyer of wisdom and discrimination."

Again in *Verses 70* and *71* of *Chapter II* the Gita tells us not to cultivate desires but insists on abandoning them.

Verse 70 – Chapter II

"He unto whom all desires enter as waters into the sea, which though ever being filled is ever motionless, attains to peace and not he who hugs his desires."

Verse 71 – Chapter II

"He who abandons all desires and acts free from longing, without any sense of mineness, he attains the peace."

Thus desire which acts like enemy within must be abandoned and not nurtured. Freedom from all selfish desires leads to eternal peace.

Let us now discuss how we should deal with desires in everyday life.

In our daily life one should start with restricting desires to the level of necessities. One should not expand the field of desire and attend to only those which have to be satisfied as a matter of duty. As a general rule, all unnecessary cravings have to be curbed. As thoughts originate in the mind, it is in the mind where necessary control has to be exercised. One must think over the impending dangers which lurk in desires and therefore must reject them at the very start.

Firm mental discipline is very essential in curbing desires. One must not yield to his desires. Again continuous satisfaction of desires, with a view to getting rid of them, will not end desires. However, the suppression of desires is also not the right way, as suppressed desires are bound to come back with greater strength. One should therefore exercise firm control rather than satisfy or suppress them. The solution lies in right thinking and proper understanding of the consequences of having these desires. Strong determination and repeated reminders are helpful in curbing desires.

Let us consider how desires play their role in our daily life. Take the example of eating tasty spicy food or sweets or ice cream and so on. When you eat it for the first time and like it, you will like to eat the same stuff again and again. If it becomes a habit it can lead to health problems. Similarly one develops strong liking for other items which include money, dresses, sex, viewing films etc. Thus one may cultivate desires for fame, wealth, eating and drinking etc. So long as desires are legitimate requirements, it is all right but when these become a craze and go beyond a desirable limit, problems are bound to arise. Bad habits of smoking and drinking, addiction to drugs are some common examples.

Desire is caused because there is something to seek, to acquire from some external source. Generally, we seek comfort and pleasure, something which is to our liking. But when we cross a reasonable limit, these desires become greed and lead to disappointment and anger, if not satisfied. Material desires often become a barrier which separates man from God. Therefore, desires should be cut-down, reduced or eliminated, if possible. This would be possible if we watch our thoughts, distinguish between good and bad thoughts with the help of wisdom and thus exercise control over our senses, mind and desires. The best way to curb desires is to divert our attention from material desires to divine desires. The ultimate solution is given in the following *Verses* of *Chapter III* of the Gita :

Verse 42 – Chapter III

"The senses are great, greater than the senses is the mind, greater than the mind is intelligence, but greater than the intelligence is He."

Verse 43 – Chapter III

"Thus knowing Him, who is beyond the intelligence, steadying the lower self by the self, stifle the enemy in the form of desire, so hard to get."

As mentioned in the Gita, desire is a constant foe of the wise, sinful destroyer of wisdom and discrimination, the enemy within and is hard to overcome. A step by step approach to raise the level of our awareness is necessary. We have to go beyond the level of senses, mind and even intelligence and seek the help and guidance of the Supreme.

The motto in our daily hope should be:
"Do not let desires rule your life."

God and Nature

According to the Gita, God and Nature are not separate. Nature emanates from God and has two aspects—lower and higher. The lower nature is eightfold, as stated in *Verse 4* of *Chapter VII* of the Gita, as follows:

Verse 4 – Chapter VII

"Earth, water fire, air, ether, mind, understanding and self-sense (ego)—this is the eightfold division of My nature."

These are the forms which unmanifested nature of God, takes upon its manifestation, in the universe. This expands further into twenty four factors, as mentioned in *Verse 5* of *Chapter XIII* as follows:

Verse 5 – Chapter XIII

"The great elements, self-sense, understanding as also the unmanifested, the ten senses and mind and the five objects of the senses."

The twenty four factors mentioned above are as follows :

- Five gross elements—earth, water, fire, air and ether.
- Four other factors are the mind, intellect, ego and the unmanifested—the latter includes mental impressions gathered as a result of previous interactions of sense-objects.
- The ten senses include five sense organs (eyes, ears, nose, tongue and skin) and five organs of action (hands, tongue, feet, and two organs of excretion).

- Five objects of the senses include sight, smell, taste, sound and touch.

The material nature, as described above is the Lower Nature of God. Besides this, there is Higher Nature of God, as stated below :

Verse 5 – Chapter II

"This is my lower Nature, know my other and higher anture which is the Soul, by which this world is upheld."

While the lower nature may be identified with the material field, the higher nature represents the consious aspect which may be identified with the Soul. The higher nature is Pure Consciousness. It is the spiritual entity which enables the body, mind and intellect (which are all material) to function. It is this Consciousness that awakens and sustains all activities in the material world. The higher nature of God is the Life Principle which sustains the entire world of experience.

Functioning of the World

Verse 6 – Chapter VII

"Know that these two natures are the womb of all beings. I am the origin of all this world and its dissolution as well."

The higher and the lower nature of God functioning in unison, bring all the manifestations in the world. The world arises from God and at the time of dissolution is again withdrawn into Him. God constitutes everything and there is no other entity higher than Him. Like waves in the ocean, there is nothing other than the ocean itself. The endless waves which rise ultimately fall into the ocean. The entire creation of the universe is held toghether by the Supreme as the cluster of gems by the string. There is one and the same Supreme in all forms.

As the lower nature is activated by the higher, in the same way the material world manifests because of the spiritual factor. Thus the functioning of the entire universe takes place through the two natures of the Supreme which is the source of life and form of all beings and objects. It follows, therefore, that each individual has two aspects— conscious and unconscious and these represent the two natures of the Supreme. There is no other entity higher than this Supreme God who includes everything and effects all activites of the world.

❑❑

Functioning and Control of Mind

Mind is the fulcrum around which human life revolves. It is a very vital constituent of nature as is evident from the verses quoted below:

Verse 5 – Chapter XIII

"The great elements, self-sense, understanding as also the unmanifested, the ten senses and mind and the five objects of the senses."

Verse 42 – Chapter III

"The senses are great, greater than the senses is the mind; greater than the mind is the intelligence but greater than the intelligence is He."

In the human body, mind occupies a place above the senses but below the intelligence. There are five senses of knowledge and five senses of action. The mind acts as a coordinator between the two. Mind thinks, imagines, resolves and plans and thus plays a very vital role in the body set-up. Our wordly life is an inter-play of senses, mind and intelligence. When the mind is under the sway of the senses, it is in bondage and gets deluded. But when it is united with intelligence, there is less bondage and more freedom. The highest freedom is attained when the mind is controlled by intelligence which is suffused by the light of the Supreme. The senses by their intrinsic nature run after sense objects. In this race, they develop a liking for the respective sense object. The eyes love to see beautiful objects, ears like to listen to sweet words, songs and music, tongue relishes tasty food, nose would prefer pleasant smell. These feelings of love, liking or taste for their sense objects are created through the association or direction of the mind. Alone, senses can not develop such feelings, as they act as mere channels or instruments of the mind. Having developed these likings, the mind follows the senses and makes them run after sense objects for more pleasure and satisfaction. The mind thus becomes enslaved through the senses because of the feelings of pleasure and enjoyment which it gets from sense objects.

When the mind becomes habitual to sense satisfaction, the intelligence also does not function properly. Consequently, the person gets trapped in the vicious circle of enjoyment of pleasure and lack of it, which results in pain as pleasure is always followed by pain because of it transient nature. The following verse of the Gita is very relevant.

Verse 67 – Chapter II

"When the mind runs after the roving senses it carries away the understanding, as a wind carries away a boat on the water."

Thus if the mind runs after the senses, the understanding is distorted and lost. When the mind gets attached to the objects of sense, a desire to possess or use that object is produced. If the desire is not satisfied, restlessness and anger arise. The following verses in the Gita are worth mentioning in this context:

Verse 62 – Chapter II

"When a man dwells in his mind on the objects of sense, attachment to them is produced. From attachment springs desire and from desire comes anger."

Verse 63 – Chapter II

"From anger arises bewilderment, from beweilderment loss of memory; and from loss of memory, the destruction of intelligence and from the destruction of intelligence, he perishes."

It is therefore utmost essential to control the mind. Gita tells us the way, in the following verse:

Verse 26 – Chapter VI

"Whatsoever makes the wavering and unsteady mind wander away, let him restrain and bring it back to the control of the self alone."

In another verse of the Gita, the mind has been described as restless and difficult to control.

Verse 35 – Chapter VI

"Wtihout doubt the mind is difficult to restrain and restless, but it can be controlled, by constant practice and non-attachment."

Thus the Gita shows the way to control the mind. The mind is restless, ever changing and extremely fast moving. It is the fastest moving entity— faster than even the speed of light. Therefore, it is extremely difficult to control it. However, constant long practice and an attitude of non-attachment are the essential tools to control it. Both the mind and the senses have to be trained to exercise restraint vis-a-vis external influences. This is the process of Yogic Sadhna. The Gita also describes the technique of meditation—which is covered in a separate chapter of this book.

Thoughts and ideas flow through mind endlessly. Sense organs clutter our mind with the images of material world and past impressions. This state of flux of mind leads to suffering. The control of mind brings inner peace and happiness and end of all sorrows. The following *Verses* in *Chapter II* of Gita support this contention.

Verse 64 – Chapter II

"But a man of disciplined mind, who moves among objects of senses, with the senses under control and free from attachment and aversion, attains purity of spirit."

Verse 65 – Chapter II

"And in that purity of spirit, there is produced for him an end of all sorrow; the intelligence of such a man of pure spirit is soon established in the peace of the self."

Meditation

Meditation is the process to control the mind through concentration on a single point, object or thought or idea. It is towards the end of *Chapter V*, that the Gita provides some practical hints for the technique of meditation, as follows:

Verses 27-28 — Chapter V

"Shutting out all external objects, fixing the vision between the eyebrows, making even the inward and the outward breaths moving within the nostrils, the sage who has controlled the senses, mind and understanding, who is intent on liberation, who has cast away desire, fear and anger, he is ever freed."

These verses briefly describe the method of meditation along with some conditions which are required to be fulfilled. Liberation is the goal of meditation. This technique of meditation is further supplemented in *Verse 10* of *Chapter VI*, as follows:

Verse 10 – Chapter VI

"Let the yogi try constantly to concentrate his mind on the Supreme, remaining in solitudes alone, self-controlled, free from desire and greed."

The emphasis here is on concentration and control of mind, abandoning desires and greed.

Technique of Meditation

In *Chapter VI* of the Gita, there are several verses which indicate how meditation should be actually practised, through physical and mental discipline. The gist of these verses is as follows:

"The aspirant should sit on a firm seat in a clean place. The seat should be covered with clean grass, a deerskin, and a cloth, one over the other. He should focus his mind and control his thought process. He should hold his head and neck erect and his body straight and still. Without allowing his eyes to wander, he should fix his gaze on the tip of his nose. In this manner, he should sit harmonised, with his mind turned towards God."

The above technique, more or less is similar to Patanjali's yoga discipline, which consists of complete contol of mind. The human mind, because of attraction of senses to their objects, is always turned towards the external world. It has to be trained and turned inward through the technique of meditation. This is possible only through long practice (*abhyasa*) and in a spirit of non-attachment (*vairagya*). The mind has to be deprived of all sensual desires, by diverting attention from external objects and by wholly applying itself towards God consciousness. This process may be called *dhyana* or meditation. In this process the level of consciousness is raised from the ordinary waking state to the highest level when it establishes contact with the Supreme consciousness.

In *Chapter VI*, the Gita lays down some specific conditions for achieving progress in this path. These may be briefly summarised as follows:

1. The aspirant must be free from desires and longings for possessions.
2. It is essential to observe *brahmacharya*. While total abstinence from sex-indulgence may be difficult for a householder, he must control and regulate his sexual desires.

3. One must practise moderation in eating, sleep and other recreative activities.
4. Firm faith in God is utmost essential.
5. Practise restraint in all walks of life.
6. There should be fixed place and time for meditation.
7. One should sit in the right posture in which one can sit, undisturbed, for a long time.

The process of meditation requires complete self-control and the mind should be kept free from selfish and unnecessary desires. This is a difficult discipline which needs long practice and a proper mental attitude. The Supreme happiness can be achieved only when the mind becomes peaceful, pure and without passions.

Incarnation of God

"Whenever there is a decline of righteousness and rise of unrighteousness, then I send forth Myself (incarnate)."
Verse 7 – Chapter IV

"For the protection of the good, for the destruction of the wicked and for the establishment of righteousness, I come into being from age to age."
Verse 8 – Chapter IV

The above verses of the Gita indicate that God incarnates from age to age, for protecting the righteous and destroying the wicked and upholding the righteousness whenever it is in decline, or whenever the need arises. It is implied that the Supreme though unborn and imperishable, takes human form in order to destroy evil forces and to protect the good. Thus he assumes birth to re-establish righteousness. This gives rise to the theory of incarnation or *avatars*. The greatest examples are Lord Rama and Lord Krishna who assumed human forms, fought with evil forces and destroyed them for the protection of the good and virtuous.

These verses indirectly establish that God is on the side of the righteous and the virtuous and ultimately destroys the wicked and evil. It, therefore, means that we humans should follow the path of righteousness in our lives.

Selected Memorable Verses

The Gita contains 700 verses, some of which are repetitive of same thought which is expressed in different ways in order to stress its importance. It may be beneficial to read certain significant verses again and again and to reflect on them so that their real significance is properly understood. Understanding the true philosophy of the Gita is not an easy task. In order to make this process easy, we are quoting below some selected verses which are comparatively more significant and memorable. The reader will do well to study these verses and try to imbibe their true spirit.

Chapter I

Most of the verses here describe the battle scene at Kurukshetra. Some noteworthy verses are given below:

Arjuna says :

"The sight of assembled, my own people eager to fight make me tremble. My mouth gets dry and my limbs shiver."
[Verse 29]

"My bow slips from my hands and I fear my skin is burning and I am unable to stand." *[Verse 30]*

"I see evil omens and I do not see any good in the killing of my own people in this battle." *[Verse 31]*

"So it is not right that we slay our kinsmen. How can we be happy, if we kill our own people."   *[Verse 37]*

The above verses, spoken by Arjuna, show the sad state of despair and dejection, at the prospect of killing his own relatives. He is confused and indecisive, refuses to fight and therefore looks to Lord Krishna for guidance.

"Having spoken this in the battlefield, Arjuna, sad and dismayed, casting away his bow and arrow sank down on the seat of his chariot."   *[Verse 47]*

These verses provide the background for the discourse of Lord Krishna.

Chapter II

Lord Krishna comes to the rescue of Arjuna who is gripped with despair, fear and anxiety.

Lord Krishna says:

"Yield not to the unmanliness, as it does not befit you. Get rid of this petty faint heartedness and arise."   *[Verse 3]*

"You grieve for those whom you should not grieve for and yet you speak like a wise man. Wise men do not grieve for the dead or for the living."   *[Verse 11]*

"Never was there a time, when I was not, nor you and other nobles, nor will there ever be a time hereafter, when we all shall cease to be."   *[Verse 12]*

"As the soul passes in this body through childhood youth and age, even so is its taking on of another body. The sage is not perplexed by this process."   *[Verse 13]*

In the above verses, Lord Krishna tells Arjuna about the reality of life and advises him not to grieve as life always continues. The soul is immortal and passes through different stages.

"Contacts with their objects give rise to cold and heat, pleasure and pain. They come and go and do not last forever, these learn to endure." [Verse 14]

"He is never born, nor does he die at any time, nor having come to be, will he again cease to be. He is unborn, eternal, primeval. He is not slain when the body is slain." [Verse 20]

"Just as a person casts off worn-out garments and puts on new, even so does the embodied soul casts off worn-out bodies and takes on new ones." [Verse 22]

"Weapons do not cleave this self, fire does not burn him, water does not make him wet, nor does the wind make him dry." [Verse 23]

The above verses speak about the immortality of the soul. After death, the individual soul takes on a new body.

"Treating alike pleasure and pain, gain and loss, victory and defeat, then get ready for battle. Thus you shall not incur sin." [Verse 38]

"To action alone, you have a right and never at all to its fruits; let not the fruits of action be thy motives, neither let there be in you any attachment to inaction." [Verse 47]

Verse 47 above, lays down the basis of Karma Yoga. One must perform his duty in the best possible manner and accept the result of his efforts, whatsoever, without complaint or remorse. However, he should not be lazy in making efforts.

"Fixed in yoga, do your work, abandoning attachment, with an even mind in success and failure, for evenness of mind is Yoga." [Verse 48]

The above verse gives a wonderful formula for performing action with an even mind.

"When a man dwells in his mind on the object of sense, attachment is produced. From attachment springs desire, which leads to anger."   **[Verse 62]**

"From anger, arises bewilderment and this causes loss of memory leading to destruction of intellect, causing downfall of the individual."   **[Verse 63]**

"One who keeps the senses under control, remains free from attraction and aversion, attains the purity of the spirit."   **[Verse 64]**

The above *Verses 62 to 64* indicate how attachment leads to the destruction of the individual while control over senses leads to the purity of the soul.

"He, who abandons all desires and acts free from longing, without any sense of mineness or egotism, he attains to peace."   **[Verse 71]**

This verse shows that abandonment of desires is the key to the peace of mind.

Chapter III

"In this world a two-fold way of life has been taught by Me, the path of knowldege for men of contemplation and that of works for men of action."   **[Verse 3]**

"The senses are great, greater than the senses is the mind, greater than mind is intelligence, but greater than the intelligence is He (the self)."   **[Verse 42]**

These verses indicate the level of importance of the constituents which make our life. The soul is above the senses, mind and intelligence and the Supreme is above all.

Chapter IV

"Whenever there is decline of righteousness and rise of inrighteousness, I send forth Myself."   **[Verse 8]**

"The Supreme, though unknown and undying incarnates himself in human form, from time to time, to uphold righteousness and to destroy wickedness." [Verse 9]

Chapter V

"One should not rejoice on obtaining what is pleasant nor sorrow on obtaining what is unpleasant. He who is stable in understanding and unbewildered is established in God." [Verse 20]

"Whatever pleasures are born of worldly contacts are sources of sorrow, they have a beginning and an end and no wise man delights in them." [Verse 22]

All pleasures of mundane life seem pleasant but end in sorrow. It is not wise to revel and delight in them.

"He who finds happiness within and is content in self, he becomes divine and attains to the beatitude of God." [Verse 34]

This verse indicates that the peace of mind and divine bliss lie within and not in external objects.

Chapter VI

"Let a man lift himself by himself; let him not degrade himself. He himself is his friend and foe." [Verse 5]

The above verse teaches the way of self-development which lies in self-effort. If we exercise self-control, the self becomes a friend, otherwise foe. This thought is further developed in the following verse.

"For him who has conquered his lower self by the higher self, his self is a friend but who has not done so, the self acts like an enemy." [Verse 6]

This verse stresses the importance of self-mastery in life.

"Let the yogi try constantly to concentrate his mind remaining in solitude, self-controlled, free from desires and attachment."   *[Verse 10]*

"The man who is temperate in food and recreation, who practises restraint in his actions, acquires self-discipline which removes sorrow."

[Verse 17]

These verses indicate the technique of self-discipline through self-restraint.

"Supreme happiness comes to the yogi whose mind is peaceful, whose passions are at rest, who is free from sin and has become one with God."   *[Verse 27]*

Peace of mind is essential for God-realisation.

"Without doubt the mind is restless and difficult to restrain, but it can be controlled, by constant practice and non-attachment."   *[Verse 35]*

Chapter VII

"Earth, water, fire, air, ether, mind and understanding and self-sense—this is the eight-fold division of my nature."

[Verse 4]

"This is My lower nature. My higher nature is the soul by which this world is upheld."   *[Verse 5]*

"Everything originates from these natures. And I am the origin of this world and its dissolution also." *[Verse 6]*

These verses show that God includes all that is conscious and unconscious—in totality. He is the origin of everything which is again withdrawn into Him, at the time of dissolution.

"There is nothing whatsoever that is higher than I. All that is here is strung on Me, as rows of gems on a string."
[Verse 7]

All constituents of creation are manifestations of God and are held together by the force of God.

"The devotees of God are of four types : the man in distress, the seeker of knowledge, the seeker for wealth and the man of wisdom." *[Verse 16]*

"Of these, the wise one, who is in constant harmony with Me and is single-minded in devotion is the best—I am extremely dear to him and so is he to Me." *[Verse 17]*

Among the four types of devotees of God, the wise one who asks for nothing and is truly devoted to Him, is the best of all.

Chapter VII

"Always remember Me and fight, with your mind and understanding, set on me, you will, no doubt, come to Me." *[Verse 7]*

"He who constantly meditates on Me and no one else, ever steadfast, reaches me easily." *[Verse 14]*

Chapter IX

"On Me fix thy mind, to Me be devoted, worship Me, rever Me, thus having disciplined thyself, with Me as thy goal, to Me you shall come." *[Verse 34]*

Chapter X

"I am the origin of all : from Me, the whole creation proceeds. Knowing this, the wise worship Me with devotion and reverence." *[Verse 8]*

Knowing God as the cause of all creation, one should worship Him.

"Those who worship Me with consistent devotion and love, I grant them concentration of understanding by which they reach Me." [Verse 10]

Constant love and devotion to God are the means to reach Him.

Chapter XI

"By unswerving devotion to Me, I can be known, truly seen and entered into." [Verse 54]

"One who performs all his actions for Me, who considers me as his goal and worships Me, free from attachment and without ill-will to all creatures, attains Me." [Verse 55]

Chapter XII

"Fix thy mind an Me alone, let your understanding dwell on Me. Then you will always be with Me." [Verse 8]

"Those who have full faith in Me and holding me as their supreme aim, follow my immortal wisdom are exceedingly dear to Me." [Verse 20]

Chapter XIII

"Nature is the cause of the effect, the instrument and agency, while the soul is the cause of the experience of pleasure and pain." [Verse 20]

"The soul being amidst nature, enjoys the modes of nature, gets attached to them and due to this association, takes birth with these traits." [Verse 21]

According to this verse, birth takes place in different forms of life on the basis of attachment of the soul to modes of nature.

"Some perceive the self in the self by the self through meditation, others through the path of knowledge and still others by the path of action."   *[Verse 24]*

The above verse indicates the three paths of God-realisation.

"One who sees that all actions are performed only by nature, and not by self, he sees the real truth."
[Verse 29]

The soul is not the doer but only the witness.

Chapter XIV

"The three modes (gunas)—goodness (SATTAVA), passion (RAJAS) and dullness (TAMAS), born of nature, bind down in the body, the imperishable dweller in the body."
[Verse 5]

The three gunas or tendencies of human nature influence the soul when the latter identifies itself with the former. In this way, the soul gets in bondage. In order to get out of bondage, the soul has to rise above the hold of gunas.

"Goodness brings happiness, passion leads to action but dullness, veils wisdom and attaches to negligence."
[Verse 9]

The three modes are present in all individuals in different degrees. The prevailing mode has its consequences accordingly, as mentioned in the above verse.

"When the embodied soul rises above these three modes that spring from the body, it is freed from birth, death old age and pain and attains life eternal."
[Verse 20]

One has to rise above these modes, in order to attain liberation.

"He who serves Me with unfailing devotion of love, rises above the three modes is fit for liberation."

[Verse 26]

The way to rise above three modes lies through love and devotion of God.

Chapter XV

"A fragment of My own self, having become a living soul, eternal in the world of life, draws to itself the senses of which the mind is the sixth, that rest in nature."

[Verse 7]

The soul in the individual is a fraction of God. When it is in the body, it associates with the mind and the senses, which are born of nature.

"There are two persons in this world, the perishable and the imperishable. The perishable is all the existence and the imperishable is the unchangeable."

[Verse 16]

God is unchanging and imperishable while the material objects are perishable.

Chaper XVI

"There are two types of beings created in this world-the divine and the demoniac."

[Verse 6]

Broadly speaking, all beings created in this world can be divided into two types—the good and the bad.

"Lust, anger and greed are the gates to hell and these ruin the soul. One should avoid these."

[Verse 21]

Chapter XVII

"Good men (SATVIK) worship God, the passionate (RAJSIK) worship the demigods and the dull (TAMSIK) worship the spirits and ghosts (forces of darkness)."
[Verse 4]

Influenced by three gunas individuals conduct themselves accordingly.

Chapter XVIII

"All dutiful actions ought to be performed giving up attachment and desire for fruits."
[Verse 6]

The Gita insists not on renunciation of actions but on performing duties with renunciation of desire for fruits of such actions.

"It is indeed impossible for any embodied being to abstain from work altogether. But he who gives up the fruit of action, he is said to be the relinquisher."
[Verse 11]

Everyone has to perform some action. The true relinquisher (*sanyasi*) has no desire for fruits of his actions.

"An action which is obligatory, which is performed without attachment, without love or hate by one undesirous of fruit, that is said to be of 'goodness'."
[Verse 23]

The above verse indicates how good actions are performed.

Chapter XVIII

"That happiness which is like poison at first and like nectar at end, which springs from a clear understanding of the SELF is of the nature of 'goodness'."

[Verse 37]

The above verse defines happiness for which one should aspire.

"He from whom all beings arise and by whom all this is pervaded — by worshiping Him through the performance of his own duty does man attain perfection."

[Verse 46]

True worship of God lies in the true performance of one's duty and this is the means to attain perfection.

"Fix thy mind on Me, be devoted to Me, sacrifice to Me, prostrate thyself before Me, so shall thou come to Me, I promise thee firmly, for thou are dear to Me."

[Verse 65]

"Abandoning all duties, come to Me alone for shelter. Be not grieved, for I shall release thee from all evils."

[Verse 66]

The above verses show the way to reach God through devotion and complete surrender to Him.

A Summary of Prominent Teachings of The Gita

Chapter I
- The battlefield of Kurukshetra has been described as the field of righteousness. Our life is also like a battle. This battle should be fought on moral principles — as a struggle between good and evil.

Chapter II
- Do not be dejected in any crisis. Have courage and face it.
- Do not yield to cowardice when faced with challenges of life.
- Do not grieve in any situation of life. Wise men do not grieve for the dead or for the living.
- Pleasure and pain are transitory — They come and pass away. Learn to endure them.
- The soul is imperishable, it is the body which dies, Life continues forever.
- Do not grieve over death as it is inevitable. It is also a doorway to another life which never ceases to be.
- Do not falter in your duty.
- Fight your battle of life, with an even mind, in pleasure and pain, gain and loss, victory and defeat.

- Perform all actions as a duty and without concern for their results.
- Have faith in God and perform your duty in a disciplined and intelligent manner.
- Remain content and free from unnecessary desires.
- Avoid fear, anger and passionate desire for objects of senses.
- Keep your senses under check and mind free from attachment and aversion.

Chapter III

- Do not shirk work/action, as action is better than inaction.
- Perform action, free from attachment and keeping God in mind.
- Control your desires with the aid of true knowledge and wisdom.
- Always remember God.

Chapter IV

- Remain free from fear, anger and passion and keep thoughts of God within you.
- Do your duty, free from selfish desire and attachment to the fruits of action.
- Remain content in all circumstances.
- Learn by inquiry, humility and service.
- Subdue your senses and have firm faith in God.

Chapter V

- Perform actions without attachment and offering them to the Supreme. Action in a detached spirit is renumeration.
- Do not delight much in pleasures as they are source of sorrow.

- Resist the rush of anger and desire.
- Find happiness within, in the consciousness of God in you.
- Do good to all creatures.
- Do not rejoice too much in pleasant situations, nor feel sorrow in unpleasant ones.
- Control your mind, senses and understanding — cast away unnecessary desires, fear and anger and meditate on God. This is the path to God realisation.

Chapter VI
- Disciplined activity, without seeking its fruit is renunciation.
- Conquer your lower self (material nature) by the higher self (spirit).
- Remain equal-minded among friends and foes.
- Remain free from desires and longing for possessions.
- With focused mind, practise meditation on God.
- Practise brahmacharya — regulate and restrain your sex-life.
- Do not eat too much or abstain too much from eating.
- Exercise restraint in all walks of life.
- Restrain your wavering and unsteady mind and try to fix it on the thought of God.
- Worship God with full faith and devotion.

Chapter VII
- God is the origin of all this world.
- God is both nature and spirit — there are lower and higher natures. The material world is the lower manifest nature.

- Worship God with single-minded devotion.
- Take refuge in God and seek deliverance from all sorrow.

Chapter VIII
- Remember God at all times.
- God is the Supreme Person — the imperishable. He can be reached by constant practice of meditation and unswerving devotion.

Chapter IX
- Feel the divine presence everywhere and in all beings.
- Fix your mind on God and worship Him with full devotion and self-discipline.

Chapter X
- Remember God as the source of everything and of all virtues and all true knowledge. Worship Him with love and devotion.

Chapter XI
God is the goal. Love all creatures and seek His grace, through humility and unswerving devotion.

Chapter XII
- Fix thy mind on God, with full understanding.
- Practise concentration.
- Perform all actions for the sake of and as service to God.
- Take refuge in God and in all humility renounce the fruit of all actions.
- With full faith in God, have Him as your supreme goal.

Chapter XIII
- Try to understand Nature, Soul (individual) and the Supreme Soul and their roles.

Chapter XIV
- The 3 modes of nature are — *Sattava* (goodness), *Rajas* (passion) and *Tamas* (dullness). Try to rise above them in order to reach God.

Chapter XV
- Try to know God.

Chapter XVI
- Acquire divine qualities and discard the demoniac. In other words be good, do good and shun evil.
- Abandon lust, anger and greed — these are three gateways to hell.

Chapter XVII
- Try to understand various phenomena of life on the basis of three modes of Nature and practise the Sattava mode.

Chapter XVIII
- Perform actions with an attitude of renunciation of desire and do not renounce actions (duties).
- Give up desire for and attachment to the fruits of action.
- Do your duty with full devotion and strive for perfection.
- Do work suited to your nature.
- Practise restraint in all walks of life. Exercise control on speech, body and mind. Love solitude, eat less and perform duties, taking refuge in God.
- Surrender completely to the will of God.

Epilogue

Man is at the top of all creation. He has the physical and mental framework, the capacity and intelligence to perform and achieve what other living species can not.

Inspite of all these privileges, the entire world is in turmoil. Ironically, the conditions are more pathetic in India, the land of origin of the Gita.

Inspite of the spiritual knowledge as contained in the Gita, being available here, our country is in a pitiable state, bedevilled with evil practices and happenings, surrounded by apathy, poverty, hunger, injustice, ignorance, deficiency and disease. Even in, so called, modern, developed, educated and progressive circles, there is surfeit of selfishness, greed, anger, infight, stress and other moral deficiencies. In general, humanity at large is more or less, in a state of unhappiness inspite of various means of modern and material life at their command. Even among the richest no one can say that he is perfectly happy or fully satisfied with their present day existence.

Man creates his own world of pleasure and pain, comfort or discomfort, virtues and vices, through his desires and inherent-basic tendencies which consitute his lower nature. But he is endowed with a higher nature too, which has the potential of turning vices into virtues, pain into pleasure and true happiness.

This transformation can take place by self-effort and proper spiritual guidance as contained in scriptures, such as, the Gita.

Our material worldly life is motivated by desires. Constant contacts with the material objects lead to attachment, which produces an urge to acquire. When a desire is fulfilled, we crave for more and more, endlessly. A desire unfulfilled leads to dissatisfaction and anger. Anger produces delusion followed by loss of reasoning faculty and collapse of intellect and total failure or fall of man! We must remember that desires are never satiable.

The various divine virtues, as described in the Gita make a person worthy, strong, peaceful and purposeful. All these lead to wisdom and true understanding. Having studied, understood and realised the importance of the teachings of the Gita, one must ponder. 'How to reach the perfect stage which transcends all misery!' The Gita indicates the practical paths of yoga of Action, knowledge and devotion and the method of meditation by which the final goal of life can be achieved. These paths are not separate watertight compartments. The practical approach lies through practice of a synthesis of all these yogic paths. Selfless action, right knowledge and firm devotion, all these have to be performed and acquired simultaneously, in all walks of life. All these paths lead to the same goal, the adoption of a particular yoga in a lesser or greater degree depends only on the attitude of a practitioner.

A few last words of caution to remember! The Gita is not meant just for reading or reverence only. The message which it gives, the lessons which it teaches are essentially meant to be practised in every day life. As Swamy Parthasarthy has said:

"The Gita is a plan for Action, not for retirement."

The Gita warns about the pitfalls of material life and also shows the way to rise to the highest goal. It is for us to make a choice.

❏❏

Other Books on Religion

The Yoga of Gita

—*Dr Ram Shanker Tiwari*

Scriptural guidelines to success, serenity, harmony & happiness

The Bhagavad Gita is replete with universal wisdom and the techniques to attain this. **The Yoga of Gita** contains the essence of this wisdom, the philosophy of creation and the Ultimate Reality, as revealed by Sri Krishna to Arjuna. The book outlines the various paths for realisation. For the layman, the emphasis is on the Yoga of Action – acting without worrying about the rewards for our actions.

The book is a rendition of the 18 chapters, retold in simple language, with a brief account on Yoga and Meditation, which will ensure success, serenity, harmony and happiness for readers, who follow these principles, finally leading to Salvation.

Size: 5.5" x 8.5" • *Pages: 156* • *Price: Rs. 80/-* • *Postage: Rs. 15/-*

Know the Vedas At a Glance

—*Dr. Raj Kumar, PhD*

A clear and concise account on select aspects of the Vedas to gain true knowledge, solve problems of every kind and ensure peace, prosperity and happiness.

The scriptures and classics of a nation are its true heritage, laying a firm foundation for its people to follow. The Vedas are India's and the world's oldest scripture, believed to have been directly revealed by God.

Know the Vedas at a Glance gives a clear and concise account on select aspects of the Vedas, which help dispel ignorance, superstition and false beliefs. The Vedas are replete with guidelines to solve varied problems – social, economic, political, scientific, mental or any other. The message of the Vedas holds relevance for the layman as well as scientists, politicians, educationists, parents and people of every hue. Understanding and following the essence of the Vedas ensures a happy, healthy, peaceful and prosperous life.

Size: 5.5" x 8.5" • *Pages: 136* • *Price: Rs. 80/-* • *Postage: Rs. 15/-*

Other Books on Religion

Know the Upanishads

—*Ramanuj Prasad*

Like the proverbial fish that has heard a lot about the great ocean and spends an entire lifetime searching for it, not realising it has always been an inseparable part of the ocean, man spends his lifetime searching all around for God. All man has to do, in fact, is to simply turn his gaze inwards to realise that God or the Self has always been an inseparable part of him.

The Upanishad tells man that he is not a mere mortal, but a part of the Immortal One. **Know the Upanishads** shows you just how to go about uncovering the layers of ignorance and illusion to realise your true nature – the Self. This is the path to *moksha* or *nirvana* (liberation), which every seeker wishes to tread upon in order to break the cycle of birth and death. With pearls of wisdom from the Upanishads, the Vedas and the Bhagavad Gita, this book could transform your way of life forever, teaching you the true meaning of existence.

Size: 5.5" x 8.5" • Pages: 120 • Price: Rs. 80/- • Postage: Rs. 15/-

Vedantic Truth Revealed

—*Ramanuj Prasad*

A Cosmos and Cosmology Identity with the Infinite Fetters of Religion and Purity of Mind Unto the Reality

What is life? What is death? What's the reality of pain and pleasure, truth and falsehood? The eternal questions that have intrigued mankind since time immemorial have been discussed at length in Vedanta — the last part of the Vedas (Sruti).

Now this book reveals the Vedantic truth in a simple, lucid manner — educating us on how we can transcend our senses and comprehend the cosmic reality by acquiring that knowledge through which everything finds existence.

Human beings are blessed with the ability to purify themselves and attain higher consciousness. This book serves as a wake-up call to all those, who wish to cast away their inertia and follow the path of limitless joy and peace.

Size: 5.5" x 8.5" • Pages: 104 • Price: Rs. 48/- • Postage: Rs. 15/-

Other Books on Religion

Know the Purāṇas

—*Ramanuj Prasad*

An exquisite work to give true knowledge of the ancient Indian culture in all aspects of religion, myths, beliefs and practices as depicted in the epics of the Puranas.

The Puranas are the living images with breath and heartbeats and have manifestation of devotion to the duties, discipline [conduct] and identity with the Lord, who dispenses the fruits of actions. Through the constitution of heaven and hell (Swarga and Naraka), it gives jolt to the root of human tendency. Thus one is awake to one's own footsteps to guide, not to be guided blindly. Since then, much waters had gone down and many were spilled over. But the Puranas still today dare to play back the melodies of the Sun and the Moon for you.

Size: 5.25" x 7.75" • Pages: 328 • Price: Rs. 96/- • Postage: Rs. 15/-

VEDA A Way of Life

—*Ramanuj Prasad*

The Veda (Sruti) is the most comprehensive doctrine on religion ever revealed to mankind that answers all man's queries on the here and now and the hereafter. Human objectives can be broadly grouped under four categories: Desire (kama), material gain (artha), religious merits (dharma) and liberation (moksha). The Veda holds the key to fulfil all these aspirations. But the Veda simply reveals the Truth, never pressurising anyone to follow a particular path to self-discovery. Each person is free to choose his own path to discover the Self or God. The Veda acts as a means to the ultimate knowledge that is possible through direct perception.

VEDA: A Way of Life seeks to increase awareness amongst readers about this wonderful treasury of ancient wisdom. Study of this enlightening text will increase values of brotherhood, love and compassion, which are the need of the hour in our troubled times. The Vedic or spiritual way of life promoted by the Veda was later advocated by Lord Krishna through the Bhagavad Gita. This book presents basic tenets of the Veda so that mankind functions according to just eternal laws to ensure universal peace and brotherhood.

Size: 5.5" x 8.5" • Pages: 144 • Price: Rs. 80/- • Postage: Rs. 15/-